AIM HIGH

To order additional copies of *Aim High,* by Terry Lyndon Johnsson, **call 1-800-765-6955.**

Visit us at www.reviewandherald.com for information on other Review and Herald® products.

AIM HIGH

The thrilling story of an unlikely member of the president's honor guard who proved that all things are possible with God.

TERRY JOHNSSON

with Kay D. Rizzo

Foreword by Ben Carson

REVIEW AND HERALD® PUBLISHING ASSOCIATION
HAGERSTOWN, MD 21740

This book was
Edited by Gerald Wheeler
Copyedited by Delma Miller
Cover design by Bondesign
Cover photos provided by the author
Electronic makeup by Shirley Bolivar
Typeset: 13/15 Bembo

PRINTED IN U.S.A.

09 08 07 06 05 5 4 3 2 1

R&H Cataloging Service
Johnsson, Terry Lyndon
Aim high, by Terry Lyndon Johnsson
with Kay D. Rizzo.

1. Johnsson, Terry Lyndon. I. Rizzo, Kay Darlene, 1945- .
II. Title.

B

ISBN 0-8280-1879-0

Dedication

I want to thank the special people God has brought into my life:
Memory of Linda Fay Johnsson
Memory of Grazell Settles
Memory of Phillip Shulz

Living memory of my mother, Zelma Johnsson

—Acknowledgments—

I want to thank all the Seventh-day Adventist churches
that have helped make me the person that I am:

Sharon Church
Capitol Hill Church
Stone Tower Church
Sligo Church

Without any of you I could have never made it.

And finally, to the many young people by whom I have had the privilege of being called your pastor. Many of you are professionals and have families and have already made your own mark on the world.

You have all been the joy of my life.
Thank you for letting me practice the message of *Aim High!*

CONTENTS

	Preface	11
	Foreword	13
1	Can the Labels	15
2	Can the Can'ts	29
3	Detours	42
4	Dead Ends and Detours	58
5	"Stand by Me"	68
6	In His Honor	78
7	Learning to Care	92
8	Why Worry?	105
9	Dream the Dream	116
10	Beginnings and Endings	124
	Epilogue	141

Preface

I stood in silence, looking at the flag-covered casket of our fortieth president, Ronald Reagan. I recalled that only a few years earlier I had stood in the same place as a presidential honor guard in the company of the vice president, congressmen, senators, and foreign dignitaries. I could not believe my life had already made a full circle. As I pondered my presence amid such illustrious company, the irony of it struck me as never before. It seemed that only yesterday I was a little boy in the back of the classroom, wondering where God was, and thinking my second-grade life was over with because I could not read.

Since that time I have met every living president, and witnessed several inaugurations and two presidential funerals in the nation's capital. Now, just credits away from receiving a doctoral degree, I sometimes think that if I had not lived this life myself, I would not believe it.

Many times when we read stories about how God empowered people throughout the Bible, we wonder whether similar miracles could be wrought in this day and age. The resounding answer is yes! I say so freely because I am living proof that God can take someone considered useless and mold him into a testament of His power.

Perhaps you have wondered whether the power of God could work through someone like me, or maybe you know others in whom you see potential despite apparent weakness. My story is for them—and for you. The Word of God tells us in Jeremiah 29:11 that God has plans for our lives and, more important, that He has *good* plans for us. I challenge you to take this truth to heart and to surrender to His will, because surrendering to Him is the greatest victory a person can achieve. It was only after I stopped fighting with God that He was able to take full control of my life, and help me reach my true dreams. And He wants to do the same for you!

Today I challenge you to realize that no person or situation is too difficult for the power of God. So aim high with Him!

—Terry Lyndon Johnsson

FOREWORD

How can a man of God be a success in the United States military? I think that after reading the book *Aim High,* the reader will fully understand that the power of God can be manifested in any area of society. Pastor Johnsson uses a combination of professional storytelling and humor to get across the point that we all have enormous potential that can be utilized for success in any area of life in which we find ourselves. This knowledge is particularly useful to young people who grow up with a low sense of self-esteem, perhaps the largest issue that must be overcome in transforming one to a mind-set of success.

I am grateful that Pastor Johnsson has shared these very personal stories in a way that not only brings glory to God, but helps us understand ourselves better.

—Benjamin S. Carson, Sr., M.D.
Director of Pediatric Neurosurgery
Professor of Neurological Surgery,
Oncology, Plastic Surgery, and Pediatrics
Johns Hopkins Medical Institutions

CHAPTER 1

Can the Labels

THE AIR FORCE TRAINING instructor loomed over me like a desert thundercloud, his Smokey-the-Bear hat threatening my forehead. "I can't believe this. The military must be desperate to take people like you! You're the poorest excuse for a cadet that I've ever seen," the man shouted. I could feel the vibrations of his roar reverberating off my face. "Where's your bags, slick? Catch that bus home! Do you hear me? I said run, flyboy!"

I swallowed hard. Sweat beaded on my brow. I turned to blindly obey. Staff Sergeant Collier continued shouting as I stumbled down the empty street after a bus that had departed more than 30 minutes earlier. On my heels like a trained attack dog, the TI hounded me, demanding I catch the phantom bus.

"Lord," I prayed, "this can't be right. I just got here. How can this happen?"

It had been an exhausting day, from my family's tearful farewell in Portland, Oregon; the flight to the San Antonio, Texas, airport; to the long wait for the military bus that would take me and several other recruits to Lackland Air Force Base.

And now, at 1:00 in the morning, this no-nonsense, six-foot-six, 250-pound training instructor bellowing insults at me? Humiliating me before the men who would make up my squad during the Air Force training camp?

My throat closed; his words stung. "Lord, I can't run any farther. I can't!" My legs faltered, threatening to collapse under me. At the same time, a tape recording played in my memory, words affirming the training instructor's evaluation of me. Ugly words such as *useless, troublemaker, mentally incompetent, disturbed,* and *dummy* rang in my mind. Years earlier I'd heard those words from the lips of my second-grade teacher and from my classmates. Those hated words hammered out the cadence of my stride. Stupid! Stupid! You are so stupid! Where did you get the idea that you could make it in the military?

Somewhere in the course of my middle-of-the-night marathon, I realized I was running alone. My adversary no longer bayed at my heels. I paused to catch a breath, surreptitiously glancing over my right shoulder. Sergeant Collier had returned to the troops. He caught my eye and waved. "Get back here, slick. I'll let you stay for the night, but in the morning you're out of here. Got that?"

I stumbled back to where the men stood at attention. As I saluted my TI I couldn't miss the smirk teasing the corners of his mouth. "All right, men, file into the barracks. You, slick, wait here for five minutes, then come inside."

I took a deep breath as I watched the men disappear into the barracks. I eyed the imposing building that would become my home for the next six weeks, if I survived Sergeant Collier. The barracks held several units—or, as the Air Force referred to them, flights—of trainees. How would I locate Collier and my flight in the middle of the night? But of course that's what my TI wanted. He wanted to discourage me enough so that I would go home. I'd become his "sacrificial lamb." If I left, he would point to me as an example of a quitter, a pansy, a washout.

"Lord, I can't let that happen. You guided me into the military. Even my mother believes that. And You know my mother!" I thought of my mother's unwavering faith in her God and in her son. Would I let her down, disappoint her? At that moment it was a distinct possibility. "I don't know where to go, Lord. All I know for sure is that the flight went upstairs to the second floor. Please help me find my unit."

I climbed the stairs, my courage and my luggage dragging behind me. What would happen if I chose the wrong door? I could wake up the inhabitants of the entire building before finding my own flight unit. How many doors were there, anyway? I tried the door at the top of the stairs—a cleaning closet. The next door was locked. I tried each knob down the long hallway. With each knob I took a deep breath, hoping I wouldn't get into trouble for being in the wrong place at the wrong time. I released the breath when the knob refused to turn in my hand.

I began to worry that all the doors would be locked, that my TI had locked me out and I'd have to sleep on the floor in the hallway. Finally, halfway down the corridor, one of the knobs turned in my hand. I opened the door slowly and peered inside to find myself face to face with a startled Sergeant Collier. Evidently he never expected me to find my flight so soon. Recovering quickly, he ordered me to find an empty bunk and get ready for bed.

By the time I stretched out on the lumpy military-issue mattress at the far end of the room, I thought nothing and no one could keep me awake, but I was wrong. As physically exhausted and emotionally depleted as I was, my mind continued digging up painful memories long since buried. The hours dragged by slowly until my mind tired of its destructive game and allowed me to sleep. Then the dreams began.

I found myself behind a dusty furnace in the basement of the elementary school I'd attended, hiding from my second-grade teacher, Mrs. Pennyworth. Twelve years disappeared as if they'd never occurred, and I was once again a frightened, stuttering 7-year-old, too big for his age. Being one of the first African-American children to be integrated into an all-White school in Portland, Oregon, didn't help.

I had angered my teacher again. I wasn't sure how, but I had. Whenever a fight broke out on the playground, Mrs. Pennyworth blamed me, even when I wasn't involved. I hated being the first child she turned to whenever anything went awry. I hated being the class dummy who couldn't recognize anything beyond the first three letters of the alphabet. Whenever I'd try to read, the letters danced and gyrated on the page before my face. The word *saw* came out as *was,* and *dog* became *god*—but that was only if I could concentrate hard enough to detect the shape of the individual letters.

Both the teacher and the students in my class called me retarded. But since I didn't know the meaning of the term, it didn't really matter to me. However, I did hate being the last chosen for spelling bees and class projects. And I hated being the butt of her censure and the object of her disgust, even if I couldn't understand why.

I remember Mrs. Pennyworth answering a student's questions with "Terry is allowed to color during reading class because he's retarded" or "Terry can't go on the class outing unless his mother accompanies him. I don't want to be responsible for the safety of a retarded child." Then there was "Dumb old Terry ran away from school again." Her threat to an unruly child was "Be quiet, or I'll put you in the back of the room with Terry" or "I'll put Terry on your side in the spelldown this afternoon."

I lived two lives—a dummy at school and a newshound at home. I preferred the evening news to cartoons. While my mother prepared supper, I would sit at the kitchen table and watch the national news. Names such as Dan Rather, Ted Koppel, and David Brinkley meant more to me than Bullwinkle, Porky Pig, and the Road Runner.

This Terry could intelligently discuss politics and world economics with any adult that entered our home. At family gatherings, my mother loved saying, "Terry, tell your uncle Jesse about what's happening with Watergate." And I would give my uncle details on the findings that had been reported up to that time. I could also rattle off the latest stock market trends on command. Yet this Terry could seldom hold his own against the teacher's unrelenting attacks at school.

That first night at Lackland Air Force base in San Antonio, Texas, as I lay awake in the dark, listening to the snoring and mumbling of the other recruits, I became Mrs. Pennyworth's Terry once again.

As a child I passed between the two Terrys with relative ease. Yet every once in a while my "retarded" persona spilled over into my other life. The results always devastated me.

My family attended the Maranatha church in Portland. The Christmas I was in second grade, the church choir director came to the children's department to ask for volunteers to sing in the holiday children's choir. This was an important event for 7- and 8-year-olds, and the children eagerly volunteered. I raised my hand along with more than 20 other children.

The Sunday school teacher listed the names of the other children on the board but ignored my hand. When the choir director pointed me out, the teacher said, "You know, Terry's retarded. We can't use a retarded boy up front." The other kids snickered and I hid my face with embarrassment.

Hearing the teacher's remark, my cousin Yolanda marched

me out of the class and asked her father to take me home. I couldn't believe that a Sunday school teacher would do something like that to me. *How did she know?* I wondered. *Who told her I was a dummy?* Later I discovered that she was good friends with a teacher at my school—her source of information. I never enjoyed attending that Sunday school class again.

One day the public school guidance counselor sent a letter home to my mother. I'd often heard the term *retarded,* but I didn't really understand what it meant. I just knew it was something bad, something that made my mother cry. To me, the letter was just another note. I took notes home from school regularly. My teacher always had some misdemeanor to report. I tried to think of what I might have done. That day had been a good day at school. I couldn't remember doing anything wrong.

Yet, as my mother read the letter, tears slid down her cheeks. I asked her what was wrong, but she only held me in her arms, kissed the top of my head, and cried all the more. When Linda, my older sister, got home from work, she read the letter aloud. I listened, trying to understand.

Along with the familiar phrases such as *lazy, retarded,* and *mentally defective,* the letter included additional new words unfamiliar to me—*psychologist, expulsion, McClaren's School for the Mentally Disabled.*

The letter said that the school psychologist had given me the "inkblot test." When questioned, I remembered being shown cards with blots of ink on them. I have no idea what I might have said during the interview, but I remember wondering what the doctor was writing on his yellow scratch pad. Because of the answers I gave, he recommended I be removed from the Oregon public school system and institutionalized until I became of age. On my eighteenth birthday the state would decide if I were competent enough to reenter society.

That day I would never have guessed how much my life would be affected by those labels. Whenever I faced a difficult problem, every time I considered trying something new, or if I dared to dream beyond the immediate, those labels resurfaced in my mind and screamed at me. "You can't do it, dummy! You're too stupid! You're too slow."

Even after successfully completing the Air Force Police Academy training and after serving in the president's honor guard longer than any person up to that time, the labels programmed into my mind when I was a child of 7 kicked in whenever I faced a difficult situation.

After leaving the Air Force, I applied to Oakwood College, where a friend of mine attended. Excited about beginning my academic career, I went to see my assigned guidance counselor. The guidance counselor looked at my test scores from academy and precollege. "Terry, give up on the idea of becoming a pastor. You just don't have the background for it. You'll have to take Hebrew and Greek. Being dyslexic would make that impossible. You should consider working toward a certificate instead of a degree."

I shook my head. "No, God led me here to become a preacher, and that's what I'm going to become."

Her head wagged back and forth. "I'm sorry. You can't do that!"

She proved to be wrong. The greater battles took place in my mind, not in my class work. Constantly I had to defeat the labels pasted onto me as a child. But I reached my goals in record time. At graduation from Oakwood I received commendation from the president of the United States for my accomplishments. I never would have achieved that if I'd listened to the negative recordings in my head and to the words of my guidance counselor.

Later, at La Sierra University, pressure mounted on me to

complete a research paper, the last of my requirements for graduation with a master's degree. I had to get a B or higher, or I would have to retake the class the following year. Although I had received excellent grades, this one last paper haunted me. As I sat in the library with towers of reference books stacked around me, I could hear my second-grade teacher's voice again: "Terry, you're not going to make it. You're too dumb. You're fooling yourself. You've tricked these people into believing you've overcome this." I tried to block out the voice, but it continued unrelentingly. "Terry, the reality is, you are slow—retarded. You'll never be able to learn like the other students. Face it. Be satisfied with what you've already accomplished."

But my very presence there at La Sierra University was an evidence of God's blessing. From college I had begun pastoring in Oregon, where the church leaders encouraged me to take time off to get a master's degree, as other young pastors did—except I couldn't afford it. Then, out of the blue, a woman, Nona Korcek, called, asking if I would speak at her church near the university. The upshot of it was that she and her family made room for me in their home while I worked on my master's degree in youth ministries.

But that didn't make the actual academic work any easier. I stared at my blank computer screen. I could hear my second-grade peers chanting in a singsong rhythm, "Stupid Terry! Retard Terry! Dummy, dummy, dummy Terry!" *Will the nightmare ever end?* I asked myself for the millionth time.

Labels are great inventions for identifying canned goods on the grocery store shelf. A label informs shoppers whether they're purchasing peas or asparagus, carrots or creamed corn. Such information is important to know when buying groceries, but when labeling people—slow, bright, pretty, dumb, fat—the results are almost always devastating and destructive.

Can the Labels

We each begin life looking at our surroundings through the eyes of a child, innocent and eager to learn. We learn to identify the faces of our parents, the voices of family members. We learn to smile, to eat with a spoon, to drink from a cup. We discover who we are and what is expected of us.

During those early years, if we're told we're stupid, lazy, unwanted, we begin storing these negative labels for future reference. The labels shape our thinking. We grow up believing what we hear and what we experience. And while we may bury our pain deep within our memories, whenever the adult feels insecure the little child inside replays the original tape of insults recorded many years previously.

Recently I met an 84-year-old man, a wealthy professional, one of the most successful people I'd ever known, who still remembers the painful experiences he had as a 12-year-old. With tears streaming down his face he told me how his father had always called him stupid, dummy, good-for-nothing. "You'll never amount to anything," the father had told him.

"I could never please him." The man's pain showed in his face. Seventy years later this successful businessman still hurts from the labels his father attached to him. The father is dead, yet his words reach out to his son from the grave. The son had spent his whole life trying to prove his father wrong. He never succeeded, at least in the arena that mattered—the arena of the mind. Those early insults voided all his successes, and sullied all his joys.

Once while I was speaking to prisoners at a penitentiary, I couldn't take my eyes away from the face of one of the inmates in the very back of the room. After the program the man stood in line to speak with me. When I went to the back to meet him, he said, "You don't remember me, do you?"

I took a long look at his face, but no name would come to mind. "You look familiar" was all I could venture.

When he told me his name, Warren (not his real name), I remembered him. I hadn't heard him mentioned in 20 years. He'd been one of my classmates in second grade—another of Mrs. Pennyworth's labeling victims.

I asked him about his life. He told me he was doing a three-term sentence. Tears glistened in my eyes as he told me about being in and out of jail since he was 11. He too had been classified as a "difficult learner." Teachers would briefly try to work with him, but when they failed they'd pass him on to get him out of their class. When he was in the sixth grade the school system began standardized testing, and his world fell apart.

"They discovered I had a third-grade learning capability and told my parents to take me out of school and put me in a special education school." Tears streamed down both of our faces as he continued. "I knew I wasn't learning in the regular school, but they didn't have to put me into that place! Most of the kids there had severe problems. Only six out of the 31 could talk. Most of them wore diapers. The supervisors didn't trust us to use tableware. During lunch we had to eat everything with our fingers." He paused to compose himself. "I tried to tell my parents what was going on, but they believed the teachers, not me. They'd given up on me."

I heard Warren's pain in his every word. "As soon as I could, I dropped out of school. I started hanging out on the streets. That's when I got mixed up with a gambling ring and with drug pushers. I was good at both. Before long I was clearing more than $40,000 a month. I became the number one man in the city." The look in his eyes begged me not to reject him.

"The reason I was so good at what I did was that I never used paper for transactions. I did it all by memory. I added and subtracted, and kept all my accounts in my head. All types of businesspeople worked through me because they knew that if I got caught, there would be no paper evidence."

And this was the boy they said was too dumb to learn. He had to be a genius to memorize years of accounts in his head. I considered the differences between the two of us. Why had things gone wrong for him and not for me? One of the most obvious answers was our parents. Mine never gave up on me; his did.

I thank God every day for my mother. When everyone else considered me hopeless, she kept on believing in me. When the whole world told her I was a lost cause, she never lost faith. My mother placed her faith not just in me, because I, like Warren, would mess up; my mother put her faith a giant step further. She placed her trust in the power of God to work through me.

Today I often think of Warren, sitting out his young life in prison. He'll be close to 80 years old when he completes his sentence. I could have been him. He could have been me. If he'd had the same training as I, he could have become a banker or a stockbroker—who knows? Instead, the world convinced him that he wasn't capable of suceeding at anything but crime.

Any student of psychology knows that if you tell a person something again and again, the person will believe it. In frustration a mother shouts, "You're just like your father! A good-for-nothing bum!" Sooner or later her son will believe that too. There must be a thousand Warrens out there who have failed in life because no one cared enough to believe in them.

A couple years ago I met a man who lamented the fact that his son seemed to have given up on life. "He fails at every job he takes," the father said. "It's not that he hasn't had the best of everything—he has. The best of families, the best education, the best business opportunities a person could ever want. But everything he touches goes wrong. Do you think you could talk with him, possibly help him?" I agreed to try to help.

The boy was a good-looking, well-mannered 27-year-old. We talked about his life and about his schooling. When I shared my experience with him, I could see tears forming in his eyes.

"I can relate to you so well," he whispered.

I stared at him in surprise. *How can this guy understand my background?* I wondered. He had the best of everything. His monthly allowance was more than my yearly salary.

The young man continued: "My father doesn't realize how much he pushes me. He expects me to get everything right from the beginning. Whether it was learning to ride a bike or playing golf, he'd call me a loser if I did not shine. He said that if I didn't do it right I'd end up like his brother, my uncle Bob." The young man studied his hands for a moment, then continued. "I guess I heard it so much that I started giving up. When things don't work, I quit."

Later the father asked about our conversation. Before answering, I asked the father if he could think of anything that would cause the boy to give up.

"Are you kidding?" The father sneered. "That kid's had the best of everything."

I mentioned that his son had referred to an Uncle Bob. At the mere mention of Bob's name the father exploded, ranting for some time on how his brother was a born loser. "Unfortunately, my son is starting to act just like him."

"When did you first notice the similarities between your brother and your son?"

"At quite an early age."

"Really? Did the boy hang out with your brother?"

"No! I wouldn't allow that."

"Do you believe the offensive behavior is in your family genes?" I asked.

"Absolutely not! I'm not that way."

I took a deep breath and carefully brought up the problem of labeling people. The father grew angry at me.

"I would never do that to my son." The man stormed away from me. I wondered if I'd ever see or hear from him again. And I worried over the fate of the hapless young man.

A few days later the father called me. "Terry, I'm sorry for getting angry at you. You hit too close to home. I was so afraid that my only son would be a loser that I labeled him without realizing it. And now he's become like my brother! Do you think it's too late for my son and me?"

"Never!" I directed him to Mark 9:23, which declares, "Everything is possible for him who believes" (NIV).

"You and your son need to learn the art of believing—in each other and in God. If you expect the worst from people, you'll get the worst. If you practice believing the best through the power of God, the best will manifest itself."

Today the son is in medical school and doing very well. His dad is his biggest supporter, whether the boy gets a good grade or a bad one.

Many school systems regularly label children. Terms such as *slow learner, attention deficit disorder, D student, culturally disadvantaged, hyperactive,* and *at-risk child* are counterproductive to the purpose of education itself. These labels work in the brain in much the same way as "bad" cholesterol clogs the veins, preventing the healthy flow of positive education. If Albert Einstein were alive today, his student file would read "slow learner, possible attention deficit disorder." Teachers called Thomas Edison, considered by many to have been the greatest American inventor, a lazy learner.

Consider what painful childhood experiences shaped the lives of people such as Malcolm X or Martin Luther King, Jr., Mahatma Gandhi or Abraham Lincoln, Adolf Hitler or Idi

Amin. Many great individuals have succeeded in spite of society's labeling system. Many more have become murderers and scoundrels because they couldn't shake off the bad memories. The overwhelming majority of prisoners doing hard time in America's prison system today were abused as children. While the only hope for redirecting the lives of these individuals is the power of Jesus Christ, society can make a difference in the lives of the next generation. And one giant step would be to can the labels.

That sounds good, but how does one go about canning the labels that have been glued on since childhood? The first step is to can the urge to label other people, to stop thinking of others in terms of simplistic titles ("he's lazy," "she's sloppy," etc.). Labeling is a habit like any other habit. And like any other habit, it can be broken.

This is where God comes in. He's the one who promises to give you the strength to overcome. And He keeps His promises. Claiming God's promises for strength is more than practicing a Pollyanna, everything-is-beautiful, attitude. It's more than the philosophy of "If I think I can, I can."

I discovered that winning through faith in God is a premise even for those who consider themselves spiritual wimps. Without His strength sustaining me, those labels from childhood would continue to defeat me. I would never have finished academy, never have lasted in the military, never have made the president's honor guard, never have graduated from college, and never have completed my master's degree. And that's only the beginning of the rest of my life.

CHAPTER 2

Can the Can'ts

SERGEANT COLLIER'S ACCUSATIONS, mingled with Mrs. Pennyworth's hateful words, played again and again in my head: *You can't make it, Johnsson. Admit it, you're too stupid! What made you think you could succeed in the United States Air Force? Talk about dumb!* After several hours I fell asleep, only to be startled awake by the shrill predawn blast of reveille.

Clothes and epithets flew as everyone in the flight unit scurried to meet the staff sergeant's deadline. "OK, Terry," I ordered, "this is a new day. We start again. Keep a low profile. Don't do anything to attract Sergeant Collier's attention."

I bent to tie the laces on my Nike sneakers when a sergeant shouted, "We're gonna do a shakedown search! Put all your belongings on your bed. Dump your bags!" The sergeant stood in the aisle, legs spread, thumbs gripping his belt buckle. "If any of you yahoos were dumb enough to bring along any drugs or weapons, don't try to hide 'em!"

Sergeant Collier emerged from his quarters and joined the other sergeant in the search. As I unzipped my luggage, I sighed with relief. I knew I hadn't brought along any weapons or drugs from home. My relief lasted less than a minute.

"I do hope none of you are religious nuts. We had one in the last flight. He used his religion to get out of work whenever he could. I won't tolerate any stuff like that again. No excuses—got it?" I gulped and shot a hurried glance toward my suitcases. Before leaving home I'd asked my mother to pack some reading material and a Bible for me. Every Christian mother's dream request! Knowing my mother's tendency for overkill, I cautiously dumped the contents of my bag onto the bunk. Out rambled scores of books—*Steps to Christ,* the Conflict of the Ages set, magazines, and Bibles, all religious. "Bless you, Mother," I mumbled, rushing to gather them up. I glanced about hurriedly, looking for a place I could stuff them—under the bed, in the footlocker, in my jacket pockets—anywhere.

My frenzy caught Collier's attention. From the far end of the barracks, he shouted, "Stop right there, slick! What are you trying to hide? Got some drugs you were hoping we wouldn't discover, eh?"

I rolled my eyes toward the ceiling and threw up my hands in surrender. So much for keeping a low profile! Like a condor swooping down on its prey, Collier descended. He grabbed the handful of books from my grasp. "Oh, no, not again! Another religious nut case! Get this scum out of my sight!" The training instructor stormed up the aisle and into his office. By the shattering vibration of the smoked glass in the slammed door I knew the six weeks of training were going to seem a long, long time. Perhaps when he learned I was a Seventh-day Adventist he would dismiss me immediately.

My instincts were not far from wrong. From that day on, Sergeant Collier singled me out for every form of ridicule known to a military inductee. If there was a nasty job to do, I did it. I had dishpan hands and toilet bowl elbows. My knees grew calluses not only from the chores I did but also from praying for relief. More often than not, when I returned from breakfast I'd find my carefully made bunk turned upside down and my locker dumped. Collier followed his actions with taunts. "If it's too much for you, Johnsson, quit. Go home to Mama. The Air Force isn't for wimps like you."

To make matters worse, the more he harassed me the clumsier I became and the more mistakes I made. I became the laughingstock of my unit. My inability to march drew so much attention in the squad that they dubbed me "Gomer," after the Gomer Pyle character on television. Even my buddies called me Gomer occasionally.

Most of the time I could handle the good-natured harassing from my peers, and I understood Collier's attitude toward me. I knew that the staff sergeant wanted me to get angry, to blow up. This would give him excuse to write me up. My counterstrategy was to do everything with cheerfulness and dignity. I resolved to be the happiest, most cooperative flyboy Sergeant Collier had ever seen. And for the most part, my positive attitude worked. This baffled Collier more than a display of temper ever could.

One evening after a particularly grueling day on the parade ground, I thought I'd come to the end of my endurance. I believed I could take no more. Was I ever wrong!

The military behavior code for the mess hall is strict and precise. The purpose of the discipline is to teach the recruits teamwork and obedience. To be certain that military etiquette was maintained, the training instructors would sit and drink coffee at a long, elevated table called "the snake pit," and watch the recruits. Even surrounded by his peers, Sergeant Collier still managed to stand out as the toughest and meanest of the crew.

I didn't realize that Collier had learned my evening routine of hitting the salad bar immediately after going through the regular food line. My buddy and I had just completed the number of airmen required to fill a table and had sat down when Sergeant Collier bawled, "Johnsson, hurry it up. You're taking too long. Get your salad and sit down."

My face grew hot. My collar felt as if it would choke the very life out of me. I could sense the sympathetic glances of my peers as well as a few nervous snickers. My buddy glanced toward me and nodded. He'd go with me to the salad bar as required. When we reached the bar, I filled my plate with lettuce and various other fresh vegetables. Flustered with the sergeant's undue attention, I made the mistake of stepping behind the salad bar to reach one of the condiment bowls.

The instant my foot landed behind the salad bar, I heard Collier shout my name. "Johnsson!" I froze. "What do you think you're doing? Do you think this is Wendy's or something?" The other training instructors burst into laughter at his joke. "You think you can come in here and just help yourself? Get over here, flyboy!" The sergeant waved me toward the snake pit.

I held my salad bowl with both hands to control my shaking as I approached the long, fearsome table. In front of Collier, I stared at the squadron symbol mounted above the TIs' table. One of the rules was that the recruits could not look at the training instructors' table. Under my breath, I prayed as I'd never prayed before.

The sergeant bent over the table and bellowed into my face. I could feel the words vibrate against my chest. "Don't you ever go behind the salad bar again. Got that?"

Terrified, I nodded my head and said, "OK, sir." I cringed as the word OK escaped my mouth. The room grew silent. A thousand eyes stared as the staff sergeant straightened to his towering height. With determined step Collier strode around the long table to where I stood.

With hands on hips, his chin jutting forward and the brim of his Smokey-the-Bear hat almost touching my forehead, he said, "'OK'? 'OK'? What did you say, slick? Not 'Yes, sir' or 'No, sir,' but 'OK, sir'?"

I was so flustered that I compounded my mistake by dropping my tray down on the training instructors' table in order to snap to attention. Collier's icy blue eyes filled with rage. "What? Did you put your tray on our table? Don't you know you're not supposed to do that?" The man leaned forward, the rim of his hat scraping against my perspiring brow. "Do you understand me, slick?"

"O-K-K-K, sir." My eyes shot open wider as I realized I had done it again.

Disbelief swept across Collier's face. "What did you say?" He turned toward his peers and asked, "Did you hear that?"

Quick as a wink I was surrounded by training instructors, the rims of their hats ringing the circumference of my head. "Did you really hear him say that?"

The four training instructors shouted so loudly I couldn't make any sense out of their words. Inside my head I screamed, *I've got to get out of here. Run! Run!* Instinctively I backed away.

"Are you trying to walk away when your TI is talking to you?"

I closed my eyes. *Oh, Lord, I'm through. This is it. I know I'm finished!* The verbal attack continued for several minutes. *Why is this happening, Lord? I've tried to do everything You would have me do.*

After a 10-minute barrage the four training instructors turned and walked away. They stopped the harassment because they could no longer contain their laughter. I picked up my tray and hurried to my table, my hands shaking so badly that the dishes clattered against one another the way they would during a Santa Monica earthquake. By the time I reached my table, acid was rumbling in my stomach. I couldn't swallow a bite of food.

Military etiquette demanded I wait to leave the mess hall until the others at my table finished their meals. So I sat in silence, staring at the food before me and analyzing the shards of my illustrious, but short, military career.

As soon as I could do so, I rushed upstairs to my unit. I needed to get away, to be alone. I felt the way Mount St. Helens must have felt seconds before it erupted in Portland's backyard. Should one person say the wrong thing to me, I'd spew forth a river of hot lava I'd later regret.

Once I reached my footlocker, I grabbed my Bible and headed toward the door of the barracks when I heard a voice from the other side of the room. "Tough luck, Johnsson. How'd you keep from popping that guy one right in the nose?"

I cast the cadet a crooked grin. "The idea crossed my mind."

"I don't know how you put up with all the hassle that guy gives you. If it were me, I'd be on the next flight home."

I nodded. "I've considered that, too."

"You're a whole lot stronger than I am."

"Not really." I gulped, knowing the thoughts I'd been thinking. "It's not me." I held up my Bible. "Any strength I have comes from here."

I suppressed my anger for a time while we talked. When I could finally escape, I called home. My mother answered the phone. At the sound of her voice, I couldn't hold back my tears. I spilled out my horrid tale to her. When I finished, she asked, "Do you still believe God led you into the service?"

I mumbled a reluctant yes. When I enlisted, I had no doubts that God had supplied a way I could go to college without the heavy tuition costs that most four-year colleges demanded.

"Do you think He's changed His mind now, because things have gotten a little difficult?"

I knew where she was leading, and I didn't like it. I wanted sympathy, not logic.

"Remember your third-grade teacher, Mrs. Shurlock?"

Mrs. Shurlock? The teacher who'd been haunting my mind was Mrs. Pennyworth, not Mrs. Shurlock.

"Remember how often you wanted to quit when she was trying to teach you to read? You'd come home from school and say, 'I can't do it, Mommy. I can't!' "

Yes, I remembered. Of course I remembered. The ordeal was something I would never forget, no matter how long I lived. After my mother received the letter from my school guidance counselor advising her to put me in a state home for mentally challenged children for the next 10 years, she began calling schools around the country. She considered having me live with relatives, if necessary. When she'd exhausted all her leads, my mother talked with the public school principal. Mr. Bates helped her enroll me in a small Christian school near where I lived.

That's when I met the indomitable Mrs. Shurlock, a determined teacher who refused to accept defeat—from anyone, in anything. Mrs. Shurlock decided I would learn to read, and read I would. First, she switched me from reading by phonics to sight reading. She used pictures with words. Each day she assigned chapters of the Bible for my homework, then quizzed me over what I'd read. Half the time I had no idea. But she refused to give up on me. She kept me after school to work individually with me. Every time I said "I can't," she'd reply, "Yes, you can! With God you can do anything!"

Then, to reinforce her message, she had me memorize promises from the Bible, promises such as "Nothing is impossible with God" (Luke 1:37, NIV); "Never will I leave you; never will I forsake you" (Heb. 13:5, NIV); "I can do everything through Him who gives me strength" (Phil. 4:13, NIV).

Because of my past, my natural inclination was to think negatively. I was comfortable with failure. Sitting in the back of the room and coloring was much easier than trying to tame a bunch of unruly letters on a page. But Mrs. Shurlock told me that if I believed the negative labels, my fight was already over. The only way I could overcome both the negative thought patterns and my reading problem was to break the old habits. She said, "The words 'I can't' must be drilled out of your vocabulary and replaced with 'With God's help, I can!' "

Now, I grew up in a Christian home. My mother read the Bible to us. I'd heard the same positive promises many times. But they never really sank in until I began to memorize them. The more I thought about these verses, the more I believed that maybe they were meant for people like me.

Through grade school and academy other teachers added to Mrs. Shurlock's training by taking individual time with me, including Mrs. Brooks, my English teacher at Portland Adventist Elementary School; Mrs. Winters, my English teacher at Portland Adventist Academy; and Pastor Matula, my academy religion teacher. They worked to strengthen my reading and public speaking skills, as well as my confidence in myself and God. And all the way, my mother continued to support me, to tell me, "Terry, you can do anything you set your mind to."

Slowly I practiced what my mother and these educators preached. I resisted the temptation to say "I can't." I read books on positive thinking, as difficult as reading was for me. These books included several by Robert Schuller. The possibility-thinking Schuller once said, "Most people fail, not because they lack talent, money, or opportunity; they fail because they never really plan to succeed." I determined not to quit—at anything.

Situations that helped me begin to see beyond the labels I'd accrued came along. When I was in the fourth grade I came home from church one day and saw the county dogcatcher across the street on my best friend's lawn, trying to take his dog. Now, every boy in the neighborhood had a dog. And the dogs usually stayed on their own property.

I was indignant. Here was the county dogcatcher trying to take my best friend's dog. He even used a dog treat to catch the dog. How could the dogcatcher trespass on someone's property and take that person's dog? I yelled, "Run, Prince! Run!"

Prince darted around the corner of the house and out of the dogcatcher's reach. If the dogcatcher could threaten to take Prince, he could take any of our dogs. I asked my father what I could do about it, and he suggested I write to the city mayor.

Me? Write to the mayor? A fourth grader considered mentally challenged by the state of Oregon writing a letter of protest to the mayor of Portland? Mad enough to ignore the can'ts, I didn't stop with a letter to the mayor; I also wrote a letter to Senator Mark Hatfield.

My letters made me a neighborhood hero, because soon after, the mayor and the senator wrote letters to me promising to look into the practice I'd described. Later they reported back to me their findings and their steps to correct the situation. I realized I wasn't a total dud. Mayors and United States senators didn't write letters to dummies. I could make a difference. Along with this knowledge, I realized I had a keen interest in politics. It was a way I could help people.

My interest in politics grew with the presidential race between Jimmy Carter and Gerald Ford. My fourth-grade teacher wanted the class to learn about the democratic process, so she drew names out of a hat. I was chosen to represent Jimmy Carter. Jimmy Carter? Everyone laughed. "No way you're going to win, Terry. No one likes Carter. We all want President Ford to win."

Only seven in the class of more than 20 claimed to be for Jimmy Carter. What could I do? I decided I needed an edge. I wrote a letter to Jimmy Carter. I told him that I was in charge of his campaign in my class and that no one wanted to vote for him. I asked him for a list of reasons that would change their minds. I asked him what he would do differently if he were president.

To everyone's surprise, I received a personal letter from Mr. Carter. He explained why he wanted to be president of the United States and how he thought he could affect the future. The school principal called me to read the letter before the entire student assembly. When we held our classroom election, Jimmy Carter received 25 of the 27 votes.

With this fragile background of wins, I continued throughout my school years to fight the desire to quit. I joined the Air Force expecting to escape my past, until I came up against the toughest, meanest, fightingest training instructor in the United States Air Force. I didn't realize that Sergeant Collier had specifically chosen me to be his fall guy. He told the other sergeants that he planned to break me down. I didn't learn this fact until after the mess hall fiasco.

One evening as I folded my freshly washed laundry, Collier called me into his office. *Oh, no,* I thought, *what did I do now?* I dragged my feet as I headed toward his open door, searching my memory for any mistakes I'd inadvertently made. Outside of the encounter in the cafeteria, I could think of nothing. The fact that I couldn't tell my right foot from my left continued to give me hassles. But beyond that? Nothing. Terrified, I marched into the office and snapped off a salute before Collier's desk.

"Close the door."

"Airman Johnsson reports as ordered, sir!"

Collier sighed. "Forget the military, Johnsson. At ease. Take a seat. We're just going to talk."

"Yes, sir." My heels snapped against each other. All the "at ease" commands he might give couldn't put my body or my mind at ease. My stomach churned, anticipating his newest scathing rebuke.

"Forget the military, Johnsson," he said once more. "We're just going to talk."

Right, I thought, *a stun gun squaring off with a popgun.* And I had no doubt who was about to get popped. Lowering myself into the straight-backed wooden chair in front of his desk, I opened my mind to the possibility that Sergeant Collier had finally found the excuse he needed to send me home.

The sergeant sat down behind his desk. Before speaking, he cleared his throat, moved a letter opener from one side of his desk pad to the other, then straightened a stack of memos. "Johnsson, I have a confession to make to you. During the past three weeks I've done everything I could to break you."

Oh, really? Surprise, surprise! I thought. *And that's news?* My mouth tightened into an overstitched seam.

"I've been way out of line." He cleared his throat. "I wouldn't blame you if you walked right down those stairs and reported me."

I blinked.

"I can't stand it any longer. The rougher I've been on you, the more cheerful you've behaved." He paused for a moment, as if weighing his words. "What is it? Why are you so . . . happy all the time? What's your secret?"

I swallowed in surprise. This was the last thing I'd expected to hear when I entered the office. I wondered if I should tell him. Should I answer his questions honestly, knowing that he wouldn't like what he was about to hear?

"Tell me, Johnsson. I made your life miserable. How do you do it?"

I opened my mouth to speak, but nothing came out. I prayed a quick prayer: *Put the right words in my mouth.* Leaning forward in the chair, I said, "God. That's who made it possible—God."

"God?" He shook his head in disgust. "Come on, Johnsson, 'fess up. What really helped you keep your cool?"

"God." I shrugged. "God."

Collier studied my face for several minutes before speaking. "Johnsson, I did everything I could to break you. You know, you could get me into a lot of trouble for telling you all this, but it's true.

"And you never lost your cool. One swing at me, and I'd have sent you packing. Worst of all . . ." He pounded his fist on the desktop. "I can't help liking you, you and your . . . attitude."

Stunned, I stared at the man who'd made my life so miserable. As he spoke, the hurt and resentment welled up inside of me. Yes, I'd turn him in. I'd get even. How I'd love to see him swing from the yardarm, to see him blowing in the wind, reprimanded for the way he had treated me. Then Collier's words stopped me midthought.

"You're the genuine article, the real thing—a real Christian."

A-a-a real Christian? Oops. Suddenly I couldn't report the sergeant for what he'd done. I dropped my head, embarrassed for the thoughts I'd been having.

Collier explained that he'd taken a lot of harassment from his fellow training instructors during the last flight training because of a couple guys who called themselves Christians. "They used their religion to get out of doing anything unpleasant. And I vowed I'd never again become a patsy for a so-called Christian.

"If I could get the rest of the troops to adopt your good attitude, we'd win flight honors at graduation." Every unit and every training instructor at Lackland Air Force Base coveted the flight honors. "How would you like to be unit chaplain for the rest of the training program?"

I gulped. "Er, what would that entail, sir?"

"You'll still perform all the rest of your training obligations, but you'd also function as a sort of morale officer to the rest of the guys." I smiled to myself. Whether the man realized it or not, I'd already become that. His ridicule and abuse had made me a natural listening ear to the other men's complaints. When one of the men felt lonely or frustrated or needed personal advice, more often than not he asked me for help. The difference now would be that I would have a title for what I was doing.

"I'd like for you to try to get the men to attend the base chapel each week. You'll be in charge of the flight on Sunday. Wear this when you march the men to church services." He handed me an armband. "I can't believe I'm doing this. Me? Encouraging base chapel attendance? And of course you can go to church every Saturday."

In the days that followed, my marching didn't improve, and I still couldn't shoot straight enough to connect with the target board. Sergeant Collier continued to dress me down whenever I made mistakes. But knowing my training instructor was on my side made all the difference to me.

I thought about my mother's constant stream of prayers (she'd had the entire church congregation praying for me) and her wise advice on maintaining a positive attitude. I had to admit, she'd been so right. By canning the can'ts, God and I had tamed the fearsome Staff Sergeant Collier.

CHAPTER 3

DETOURS

COLLIER'S UNIT WAS ON the line for "honor flight" status at graduation. While morale and church attendance were important in the evaluation, scores for marching and target practice were also important. And a demonstration of marching would be included in the graduation exercises.

One of the recruits would have to guard the empty barracks during the graduation exercises, and a vote was taken to determine who that should be. I won that "honor" hands down. My buddies knew that if "Gomer" marched before all that brass he'd get nervous and mess up. Collier agreed. So on graduation day, with my mother attending the ceremony, I secured our barracks. Not an auspicious task, but practical under the circumstances.

When Collier returned, bearing the certificate of honor, he reminded me, "We couldn't have done it without you, Gomer." He cleared his throat and grinned. "And we couldn't have done it with you, either."

Well, that's that! I thought. *I've made it through flight training.*

The rest of the way should be a breeze. When I signed up to join the Air Force, I did so with the understanding that I would be going to chaplain school to become a chaplain's assistant. Finally I could get on with what was really important to me.

Knowing the military's ability to get things mixed up, I checked with the assignment officer to be certain I was cleared for entrance into the chaplain training program. The officer assured me that my worries were unnecessary—I had been assigned to the chaplaincy program.

My fears were put to rest until the day the bus that was supposed to take me to my new quarters stopped in front of the Air Force Police Academy. My first thought upon reading the sign was *Oh, no! What am I doing here? I can't become a military cop!* I took a deep breath. *Calm down, Johnsson. You're getting excited for nothing. For all you know, the chaplaincy school might be held on the same grounds.*

I climbed off the bus with the other flight training graduates and fell in line. The midafternoon Texas sun beat down on us and reflected off the pavement, making standing at attention uncomfortable. A training instructor strutted toward us. He announced that we'd be issued our M-16 rifles by Social Security number. He barked out the numbers one at a time. My heart jackhammered against my rib cage as, one after another, the men took possession of their weapons. *There's been a mistake! A terrible mistake, Lord! I can't shoot straight, and I can't march, remember?*

The sergeant read my number. *I won't panic! I won't panic!* I thought as I stepped forward. There has to be a simple explanation somewhere. He dropped the rifle into my hands. I stared in horror at the frightening contraption. The only gun I'd ever touched was my friend Jackie's BB gun. And all we ever did was shoot at a squirrel—and miss!

"Sir?" I said.

"Yes, Airman Johnsson?"

"There must be some mistake. I don't need a gun. Where's my Bible?" I shoved the rifle back into the startled instructor's hands.

"Your Bible?" His voice scaled two octaves. I could hear snickers coming from some of my flight training buddies. I also heard "Gomer," the hated nickname, circulating through the ranks.

"Your Bible!" The sergeant repeated.

"That's right, sir. I enlisted to train at the chaplaincy school, not the police academy. So you see, I don't need a g-g-gun. I need a Bible."

"Uh-huh!" The sergeant stared unwavering into my eyes. His gray-green eyes narrowed to pinpoints. After eyeing me for several seconds, he heaved a sigh, mumbled something about military intelligence, wiped the beads of sweat from his brow, then shouted, "At ease, men. According to my orders, Johnsson, you are right where you're supposed to be—at the police academy."

"No offense, sir, but my recruiting officer assured me that I would be placed in the chaplain training program—sir."

The sergeant shook his head and scratched his chin. With deliberate steps he strode across the roadway to where one of the other sergeants stood. They conferred for several minutes. A second and a third instructor joined them. The longer they talked, the more nervous I became. The heat from the sun intensified. I could feel the frustrated glances being sent my way from the other airmen.

Finally the sergeant returned. He shoved the M-16 into my hands. "Just take the rifle, Johnsson. We'll straighten out the paperwork later."

"Yes, sir." I swallowed hard and wrapped my fingers around the stock of the gun as I might a rattlesnake. The sergeant handed out the rest of the weapons to the other cadets, then dismissed us to our assigned barracks.

I started in the direction indicated when I heard my name being called. I saw Jeff, a friend from flight training, running toward me. "Johnsson, you still causing pain and conniptions for the TIs?"

"Guess so." I shrugged. Obviously I can't stay in the police academy."

"There's some mistake. You know the military. They'll get it cleared up in time for you to draw your old age pension."

"Thanks." I felt the weight of the rifle against my shoulder. "I would hate to kill anyone."

"Don't worry, Johnsson," Jeff assured me. "The military will work it out." Somehow my friend's assurance did nothing to reassure me. I'd seen too many military snafus since joining the Air Force to be consoled by such a promise.

I'd barely unpacked my bags when I was called to the administration building. *Ah, maybe,* I thought, *I can get this thing worked out right away.* I found the appropriate office and told the sergeant on duty about the mix-up. I explained to him all the reasons that police academy was the worst possible assignment for me. "So you see, police academy would be the last place I would want to be. I'd be useless to the Air Force."

"I understand, Airman Johnsson." The tech sergeant studied my file, then added, "You have an excellent recommendation from your training instructor." He nibbled on his lower lip for several seconds, then looked up from the file. "Why don't you stay one week while I do some checking? By then maybe we can get you shipped off to the right place."

I thanked him and returned to my barracks, certain all was right with my world.

From the two previous chapters a person may think that by refusing to quit, by canning the can'ts and the labels, life then becomes wrinkle-free. Not so. The only constant in life is change. And not all changes go according to one's wishes or desires. But God does promise that "all things work together for good for those who love God." And He also says, "Lo, I am with you always, even unto the end of the earth." Police academy seemed like the end of the earth for a wannabe chaplain who couldn't shoot straight and marched as if his shoelaces were tied together.

My first day on the firing range with my M-16 rifle I watched several other cadets step up to the platform and fire at a distant bull's-eye.

Looks easy, I thought, trying to bolster my flagging courage. *Simple, in fact.* The weapons instructor, informally dubbed "red cap," waved me forward. I stepped onto the platform and leveled the rifle at my shoulder. The stock of the rifle grew sticky from the sweat in the palms of my hands. My hand continued to shake, no matter how tightly I clutched the weapon.

Tiny rivulets of perspiration trickled down from my forehead and into my view. I wiped them away and aimed the weapon a second time. This particular firing exercise was a qualifying heat for the M-16 rifle, the first of many weapons I would need to master before completing my training in the police academy. I reminded myself that what happened out here on the firing range didn't really matter, since I was only putting in time until my new orders came through.

"Fire, Johnsson," the red cap ordered.

I held my breath and squeezed the trigger. The weapon kicked against my shoulder. Slowly I lowered the rifle. *One step at a time,* I reminded myself.

At the end of the heat the red cap tallied each man's score, then announced, "Something has happened that has never happened before, at least not since I've been at the police academy. Today, one in our group not only did not make enough points to qualify, but he never once hit the target.

A sick feeling rose from my stomach. I had no doubt he was speaking of me. "I can't believe I am doing this, but I'm going to move the target closer and allow Airman Johnsson to try again."

Heat flooded my neck and face. I could hear my fellow cadets, both friends and foes, chuckling. The nickname "Gomer Pyle" surfaced once more. The last thing I wanted was another opportunity to mess up before my peers. If only I had the promised transfer out of the unit to the chaplain training program.

Up and down the firing range people stopped to watch me try a second time. Taking a deep breath, I placed the rifle to my shoulder, leveled the barrel, fired a second round of bullets, then waited for the results.

The red cap returned, shaking his head. "I can't understand it. No one has ever missed the target that badly. Do it again, Johnsson." The weapons trainer moved the target several feet forward. I tried a third time and failed again to connect with the target.

"Sorry, son," the red cap informed me, "but you'll have to go casual."

No, I thought, *not casual.* My heart sank. This was the threat every flight instructor held over the heads of his men. For an airman in training, going casual was a kiss of death. Nothing could be more humiliating! It meant falling back a week while your friends moved on to the second phase of training. An airman going casual became a marked man. He was required to untuck his shirt and wear a special hat to distinguish him from the regular cadets. Officers and airmen alike jeered at the hapless casual as they passed. This procedure was meant to be embarrassing, as most of the casuals were there because of goofing off or getting into trouble.

I still hadn't learned that God has a purpose in everything. I was so focused on myself that I wanted to create my own perfect ending to every situation. I couldn't believe this could be happening to me. I would spend the week doing odd jobs—painting, raking leaves, emptying garbage cans. Then I would begin the training program again with a new group of cadets.

As I weeded the flower bed in front of the mess hall one morning in the blistering Texas heat, I grew angry—angry at God. Here I was, trying to do what He wanted me to do, and see how things ended up! I jammed the trowel into the sandy soil and extracted a weed by the roots. How could He let me down like this in front of my friends? How could He humiliate me like this? Hadn't I remained cheerful and optimistic throughout flight training in the face of extreme adversity?

Going casual? First, a mix-up, not even of my doing, had landed me in police academy, and now I had to go casual? I felt as if I'd been detoured from my goals. God owed me better than this! I was so humiliated. Could I ever recover'? Would I ever get to where I wanted to go?

I yanked a dandelion weed from the sun-baked earth. For some crazy reason the weed reminded me of Peter, a friend of my family, who'd been on welfare for 22 years. He and his four children lived on $600 a month. About the same time that he had started attending the Sharon Seventh-day Adventist Church he had received a letter from the state welfare department saying he was being cut from the welfare program.

He panicked and thought his life was over. He asked my mother, "Why would the Lord let this happen to me?"

She replied, "Let's pray that God is allowing this to happen for a purpose."

The purpose soon became evident when Peter got a job washing buses. Later he advanced to driving for the company, with a salary more than double my current salary.

I wondered, *Is it possible that God could have a reason for allow-*

ing me to go casual, as He had with Peter? How could such a detour work into His plan for me?

I knew about detours. Born and raised in the Pacific Northwest, I'd traveled many of Oregon's secondary highways after bad rock or mud slides had closed the main roads. Travelers would be directed onto alternate routes, often driving several miles out of their way before rejoining their original road. Would going casual turn out to be a temporary detour, or would it become a dead end?

To make matters worse, at the end of the week I returned to the administration building to discover that all the openings in the chaplain training program had been filled. If I wanted to stay in the Air Force it was police academy for me.

Devastated, I called home. Once again my mother encouraged me to give God time. He would work things out. The next morning I talked with the base chaplain. He affirmed my mother's advice. He said, "Terry, I don't believe you are here by accident or because of a paper glitch. While God's plans don't always match our plans, they will come out right if you give them a chance."

On my way back to my barracks I fought with God. He won. "All right, Lord, I'll stay in the military until You direct me otherwise. But I don't understand any of this, and I don't like it!" Somehow the "I don't like it!" made me feel a little better. I'd do what God wanted, but I'd do it kicking and screaming all the way!

The next week the red cap worked with me until I could connect with the target. I got so that I could occasionally hit one of the outer rings of the bull's-eye. "Airman Johnsson," he said after I had made a particularly good score, "I see something in you that the Air Force needs. So I'm going to do something I've never done before. I'm going to let you go ahead." He scribbled something on my score sheet. "You're only off a few points anyway. Johnsson, you're dismissed."

Off casual! I could hardly believe it. Now I could I join the newest flight of police cadets. All was right with my world once again. All was right until my first day back on the shooting range. Having confidence in my ability to shoot the weapon, the red cap commanded me to demonstrate for the new men how the M-60 worked. The moment I stepped onto the shooting platform, I knew I was in trouble. All my old phobias returned. My throat tightened with fear.

"Just squeeze off three or four shots so the men can get used to the sound the M-60 makes," he ordered.

Once, just once, I'd love to execute an order without making a fool of myself, I thought as I slipped the earphones over my ears and leveled the rifle against my shoulder. But that was not to be, at least not on this day. When my finger pressed the trigger, I froze. Open machine gun fire splattered across the firing range. I'd emptied the entire magazine. The barrel of my rifle glowed campfire red.

Unnerved by what I'd done, I stood helplessly facing the red cap as he struggled to his feet. Shaking, the training instructor stammered, "You—you're all dismissed for today."

Before I reached the mess hall for lunch, the news of "Gomer's" latest screwup had spread throughout the entire police academy. Discouraged but determined, I practiced until I qualified for the M-60, the M-16, and the M-203 grenade launcher, as well as for the .38 pistol. At the end of my training I received a ribbon for marksmanship. However, even my ribbon couldn't erase the image of the goofy "Gomer" from my reputation.

Yet I knew the truth. God showed me that what may have looked like a detour was really an opportunity to put me on the road to a miracle.

During the last week of my police academy training, my

friend Jeff told me about the tryouts for the president's honor guard. "I was wondering," he said, "if you'd go with me to the tryouts. Just come with me for moral support. I don't expect you to try out."

Wow! Everyone at the police academy knew the importance of an assignment with the president's honor guard. And as good a cadet as Jeff might be, what chance did he really have of making it? Only generals' kids and military school graduates stood a chance. I was excited just to know someone who wanted to try out for the guard.

The president's honor guard was a dream for an Air Force cadet. Less than 3 percent of the Air Force military ever got the chance to see the honor guard in action, let alone be a member of it. The lucky cadets who had served in the president's honor guard had a ticket to go anywhere in the military.

I had no intention of applying for the guard. Why add fuel for my "Gomer" fame by doing something stupid like that? So I wasn't prepared when we arrived at the academy recreation room where the honor guard tryouts were being held and the sergeant passing out application forms insisted I fill out an application as well. "If you're here, airman, you gotta apply," he ordered.

I waved my hand in denial. "No, I can't."

"If you're here, you gotta apply!" he repeated.

I threw a quick glance toward Jeff. His grin unnerved me. "Go ahead, Johnsson. What will it hurt to fill out the application? It's not as if you're seriously applying, right?"

I rolled my eyes heavenward, then shrugged. *Oh, well,* I thought, *fill out the application. There are more than 850 cadets applying. How can it hurt?* Neither Jeff nor I were ready for the announcement at the end of the day. I'd made the first cut, and he hadn't. The sergeant told us that my qualifying had something to do with a certain "look" the honor guard wanted.

On the way back to our barracks Jeff complained about his bad luck. "I guess I can blame this one on my parents, not having the right look and all." We laughed. "Imagine them choosing you for your look. Wait until they really see you in action!"

The news of my making the first cut of 400 out of 850 men traveled through the barracks. At dinner I took a lot of teasing about "Gomer" in the president's honor guard. I laughed along. It wasn't easy being the company clown, no matter how much I sloughed it off. The possibility that I'd survived the first cut seemed ridiculous to me as well. *Forget it,* I told myself. *What are the chances that I'll make all the cuts down to the magic 12 that will actually make the guard?*

I sat through hour after boring hour of the recruitment process. At the end of the second day I was surprised to find myself still in the running. And at dinner my buddies hee-hawed more about "Gomer" being in the president's honor guard. Since no one had asked me to demonstrate my marching abilities, I knew it was only a matter of time before I too would be axed.

On the positive side, I couldn't pull KP duty while participating in the tryouts. The last time I found myself on breakfast preparation, I'd pulled a major "Gomer." Before dawn I'd stumbled to the mess hall to help prepare breakfast for the pararescue trainees, the toughest unit in the Air Force. These men trained hard, fought hard, and played hard. Compared to them, all the men in the other branches of service were pansies.

My job was to load a 50-gallon plastic milk container into the milk dispenser. As I placed the fresh milk container in the machine, the pararescuer trainees arrived, hungry as wolves. They'd been out on maneuvers for more than three hours already that morning.

I hurried to line up the milk spots in the proper slots, then closed the dispenser door—or at least I thought I closed it. As I headed back to the kitchen, shouts, curses, and laughter exploded behind me. A heavy hand suddenly grasped my shoulder.

"You'd better do something about that, airman," a deep voice said.

"Huh?" I glanced up at the towering pararescuer behind me, then in the direction of his gaze. The dispenser had sprung open. Milk spewed out in every direction, showering several startled airmen. The men gyrated about, trying to escape the sprays of milk while onlookers shouted and laughed at the spectacle.

"Oh, dear God, no!" I paled.

"Here, let me help you." The stranger leaped into the shower of milk. I followed. Together we wrestled the errant container into submission, then latched the door.

"Oh, dear God," I muttered a second time as I looked at the devastation. "How could this happen?"

"Hey, it's OK," the stranger assured me, grabbing a mop procured by one of the men on KP duty. I grabbed another.

"Did you mean what you said?"

I scowled at my rescuer. "What did I say?"

"Were you really praying?"

"Absolutely! You should only know the half of it."

"You really believe in a God who loves you and looks out for you?"

"Sure. Don't you?"

The man cast me a crooked grin. "I did once."

By the time we finished sopping up the milk, the stranger had become a friend. We arranged to meet later to spend more time getting to know each other. I couldn't believe it. God had used one of my dumb mistakes to bring me into contact with one of His sons who'd somehow detoured from the way he knew to be right.

Could God do the same for me with this honor guard application? I wondered, but I dared not dream. In spite of the teasing about the impossibility of "Gomer" making the honor guard, deep inside my heart I began to wish that such a miracle could be possible. Talk about reaching for the stars! I laughed at my audacity.

On Wednesday I had a personal interview with one of the recruiters. At the end of the interview the recruiter scribbled something on my folder, attached my photo to the folder, and handed it to the sergeant seated beside him. "You're dismissed, Airman Johnsson, until tomorrow at 0900 hours."

I walked out of the building into the sunshine. I couldn't believe it. I was still in the running. That night I could hear Mrs. Pennyworth's voice in my dreams. "You're a dummy, a troublemaker. You can't do it. You're wasting your time." I awoke long before the sun, more tired than I'd been before going to sleep the previous night.

Before breakfast I took a few minutes to read a verse from Psalm 50. "Call upon me in the day of trouble; I will deliver you, and you will honor me" (verse 15, NIV). Suddenly I realized I'd been worried about bringing honor to Terry when I should have been more concerned about bringing honor to my heavenly Father. "Sorry, Father," I prayed. "Today, no matter what happens, I will honor You."

On Thursday there were only 40 men left out of the original 850. We would be interviewed by the honor guard recruitment committee. Before going in, we were each given a slip of paper containing a list of commands to execute upon entering the interview room.

My heart pounded as I read over the commands—left face, right face, about-face, and the list went on. *This is it,* I thought. My friends' predictions would finally be realized. "Gomer" would now wash out.

The interview room was like a video segment out of my worse nightmare, and my interview could have won grand prize on *America's Funniest Home Videos*. A nine-person committee—all wearing more brass than I'd ever seen gathered in one place—sat behind a long table. Each of the high-ranking sober-faced Air Force personnel held a clipboard and a pen.

I'd never been so terrified in my life. Mrs. Pennyworth's scolding face flashed before me. Her words rang in my head. *"Dummy! Dummy!"* Spots danced before my eyes. My lips and tongue grew numb. I wondered if I could be having a stroke or something.

I glanced about the room. I could feel my heart pounding from my toes to my scalp. I knew I was supposed to say or do something before I sat down, but I had no idea what. As I stood wondering what to do, the committee members glanced at me, then at one another. The captain in charge finally spoke. "Sit down, Airman Johnsson, and tell us about yourself."

I stumbled to the straight-backed wooden chair centered in front of the long table. It felt good to have something solid for support. One after another the committee members asked me questions about myself. After their questioning ran the length of the table a second time, the captain asked, "Is there anything you want to say or do, Airman Johnsson?"

Say or do? I blinked. I just wanted out of there. "No, sir," I snapped.

"Are you sure?"

I shot a glance at the row of stone faces behind the table. "No, sir, I mean, yes, sir?"

The captain cleared his throat. A slight grin teased the corners of his lips. "You're dismissed, airman."

It wasn't until I stood to my feet that I remembered the routine I was supposed to have performed when I entered the room. Maybe I could still rescue my sinking military career, I thought. OK, just do the routine and get out of here. First, salute! Right?

What happened next must have made the honor guard's list of all-time incredible bloopers and blunders. I stood at attention and snapped off a salute—with the wrong hand! Seeing the almost imperceptible quirky grins on several of the officers' faces, I peered up at my offending hand and realized I'd made a mistake. To rectify my error, I snapped off a salute with the other hand. Hearing a snicker or two, I thought maybe I'd been right the first time. So I snapped off another left-handed salute. I peered up at the hand touching my forehead. *Oh, no! Wrong hand. You salute with your right hand!* I switched hands immediately to a ripple of polite laughter.

A few more chuckles, and I was completely confused, all the while trying unsuccessfully to calm my frenzied nerves. Realizing that my salute was beyond repair, I hurried on to the sequence of commands. Left face . . . right face . . . about-face . . . left face . . . Like a whirling dervish out of control, I turned first one way, then the other, then back again, to the raucous laughter of the interviewing committee, until I lost all sense of direction and they lost all sense of military decorum.

Tears streamed down the officers' faces. Doubled over with laughter, they pounded the tabletop. One officer leaned against the wall, his head buried in his arm, and his shoulders shaking convulsively. The officer in charge looked as if he'd topple from his chair onto the floor. Another gasped for breath.

Aghast at what I'd done, I stopped short. I figured that the committee members were laughing too hard to see anything I might do, right or wrong. Every fiber of my body shouted, "Run! Run!" In barely more than a whisper I said, "Excuse me for wasting your time." Blinded with humiliation, I saluted properly, then headed for the exit.

An attractive female honor guard opened the door for me.

Too mortified to think rationally, I whispered something stupid, such as "Do you think I have a chance?"

The woman stared at me in horror, then shrieked with laughter. "Yours has to be the worst interview I've ever seen. You messed up completely—everything!"

I could hear their laughter after the door closed behind me. In all my years of embarrassment and censure, I'd never felt so hopeless and idiotic. *Mrs. Pennyworth was right.* I pounded my fist into the palm of my other hand. *I* am *a dummy.*

Instead of going to the mess hall for supper, I jogged down one of the base's seldom-used roads. How could I face my friends after such a fiasco? As I saw it, the detour I'd taken from my goal to become a chaplain's assistant was turning out to become a painful, final dead end to all my military dreams.

My emotions told me I was a loser, but my intellect reminded me that the embarrassment I felt at this moment would fade with time. What really mattered was that I not quit, that I not give up on myself or on God. While I might be at the end of my rope, I needed to tie a knot and hold on.

CHAPTER 4

Dead Ends and Detours

DEAD END OR DETOUR? That's the question I asked myself as I walked down the road to the commissary on Friday afternoon. The committee had posted the names of honor guard inductees that morning. But I had no intention of checking to see if my name was among them. Why should I add to my embarrassment by being seen in the vicinity of that list? All morning long I'd been harassed about trying out for the honor guard. In the lunch line one guy called out to me, "Congratulations for making the honor guard."

Another asked, "Aren't you supposed to be at the honor guard meeting?"

A third called across the line, "So, Gomer, when do you leave for Washington?"

"Any day now," I replied. I had the worst urge to wipe that stupid grin off the guy's face. If it hadn't been for Jeff standing behind me, I might have. I finished my meal and my day's duties as quickly as possible. All I wanted was to be alone and to buy a tube of toothpaste and some new blades for my razor at the BX, the base exchange store. And maybe a candy bar. Was that asking too much?

Lost in my misery, I plodded along the side of the roadway toward the BX, mentally listing the items I needed to purchase. I failed to hear an entourage of vehicles approaching.

"That's him! That's Johnsson." I turned when I heard the voice of my friend Chris Pardon. My mouth dropped open at the sight of four sleek black Lincoln Continentals slowing to a stop beside me. Chris's arm extended from the second vehicle's open rear window. He was pointing in my direction.

The tinted rear window in the lead car silently lowered. The sober, hardened face of a captain appeared. "Are you Airman Johnsson?" he barked.

The first thing I thought was *Oh, no, I must have done something terribly wrong this time.* But I couldn't for the life of me figure out what it might be. "Yes, sir."

"Do you know that you are the first person in the history of the United States Air Force to hold up the president's honor guard? We've been waiting for you for two hours!"

My eyebrows disappeared into my military-issue haircut. I tried to speak, but could only babble.

The captain knitted his brow in concern. "Airman Johnsson, did you or did you not apply for the president's honor guard?"

Like one of those plastic bobbing clowns, I nodded. "Yes-yes-yes, sir!"

"You are one of the seven applicants chosen, you know. Didn't you check the list?"

Bewildered, I shook my head. "N-n-n-o, sir."

The officer sighed. "Get in, son. You're going to Washington!" The door on the second car swung open, and I stumbled into the vehicle beside Chris. Once seated, I shook my head to clear the ringing in my ears, but the noise continued. I could hear Chris speaking to me, but I couldn't understand what he said. All I could think was *This can't be happening. There must be a mistake. Someone somewhere is going to discover their error, and I'll be out on my ear.* Then I thought, *No, this is a dream. I'm asleep in my bunk and I'm dreaming.*

The entourage did a U-turn and headed for the administration building. Suddenly the comments I'd received that morning came to mind. The men hadn't been harassing me. They weren't mocking me. They were congratulating me. And I thought . . . I took a deep breath and released it through my teeth. Thank God for Jeff. Thank God I didn't belt one of them.

Detour? Hardly. The detours, the mistakes I'd made, as well as the Air Force's errors, had lead to this appointment. Everything had fallen into place. Being assigned to this police academy had worked for my good. Going casual for two weeks had put me in just the right place at just the right time to be able to apply for the guard. If I'd been with my regular flight I would have left the police academy and been working in the field. *It's true. It's all true!* I smiled to myself. *All things do work together for good.*

When I talked with my folks that night, I told them about my appointment. Then I told them how discouraged I'd been, thinking I was at a dead end in my life. My mom laughed. "Terry, at your age there are very few dead ends. The entire world is before you." For the first time in a long time I believed her.

A few years later I checked my service records. I was curious to discover what the committee members had written on their reports about my interview. My file was empty. I talked with several of the committee members, but, while they remembered my performance, they couldn't remember what they'd written.

Detours and deadlines. My mom was right. There are very

few dead ends for a man of 22. But there are dead ends. I went home on furlough during my honor guard stint and ran into an old friend from the neighborhood. We laughed about old times. When I asked where several of the others from our group were, I discovered that the majority of my neighborhood friends were either dead or in prison.

The summer before I entered the Air Force, Mike (not his real name), one of our "fiercesome threesome," attended a party at which people were doing acid. Because Mike refused to use the stuff, someone thought it would be funny to drop some acid into his glass of beer. Then a second of his "friends" decided the same thing. He dropped some more of the drug into the same drink without Mike's knowing it. The double dose of acid fried Mike's mind. Today my friend's brain is so destroyed that he can barely say his own name. A genuine dead end for Mike and his family, and for the world and whatever contributions he might have made to it.

I could have been Mike. Dropping acid into Mike's drink is the kind of thing kids do to other kids. Why did this tragedy happen to him and not to me? Why is my life full of opportunity today and Mike's at a dead end? I don't understand. Yet I believe that God has both my life and Mike's in His heart. And I know that my friend Mike, despite his condition, can be a blessing in his own world if he gives himself to God.

As I prepared to fly to Washington, D.C., after the honor guard tryouts, I wondered whether my appointment in the honor guard training program was just another detour or an entirely new road God intended me to follow. Would my direction shift from becoming a pastor to a career in the military or, maybe, politics?

I'd never lost my interest in politics. It seemed like such a great way to change things, to help people who needed someone to fight on their side. My mind swam with a new set of dreams and goals never before possible.

My life had never been so exciting or so frightening. I didn't forget my penchant for making embarrassing mistakes. In the president's honor guard, if I messed up I'd mess up royally. My mistakes wouldn't humiliate only my unit but the entire Air Force, and possibly the entire country. To fortify myself, I recited the Bible promises that Mrs. Shurlock had forced me to memorize. "Lo, I am with you alway, even unto the end of the earth." For a boy from the Pacific Northwest, Washington, D.C., definitely qualified as the "end of the earth."

The city of Washington dazzled my brain. This was no dream. Everywhere I looked, I saw history being made. I craned my head out the cab window to catch a glimpse of the FBI Building, the Capitol, and the White House. I smiled to myself as I recalled the little boy who wrote to his senator to save the neighborhood dogs from the dogcatcher. I remembered how excited I'd been to receive Jimmy Carter's letter and to read it before the school assembly. *This is where it all happens,* I thought.

After receiving Carter's letter, I toyed with the idea of entering public service. But my wildest fantasies never took me beyond Portland's city hall. While I was in high school, the Portland city council organized a youth commission board. An employee of the city of Portland recommended me to represent my school. This allowed me to attend selected city council meetings; have lunch with Bud Clark, the mayor; and attend citywide youth banquets. At one banquet city commissioner Mildred Schwab gave the keynote address. In her speech she predicted that by the year 2000 I'd be mayor of Portland. The audience applauded. My friends all knew of my immense interest in politics.

And here I was in Washington, the hub of politics with all its intrigue. My life finally appeared to be on track—a different track than the ministry, but on track nonetheless. As my cab sat in midday traffic and I inhaled clouds of auto fumes, I could feel the pulsating power of the capital.

I watched businesspeople stride purposely from one building to another; and grand automobiles driven by uniformed chauffeurs honking horns impatiently in the traffic gridlock. I eyed the darkened windows of the luxury car beside me, hoping to catch a glimpse of the important person within, but could see only my own reflection in the glass.

A busload of tourists lumbered through the intersection. I grinned at the passengers' eager faces. They were so much like me, trying to see everything there was to see. The difference was that they'd be gone in a few days, and I'd still be there.

I wondered if one day the excitement I felt on being a part of the D.C. scene would dim, if my innocence would become sullied, if this moment would be swallowed up by self-importance or cynicism. Then I laughed at myself. With my track record for mistakes and mishaps, I could never forget how human I am and how great God is! Plus, I'd always have the memory of Mrs. Pennyworth to keep me humble.

The training program for the honor guard is reported to be the toughest in the Air Force. One in six trainees drops out before completing the program. A guardsman represents the United States Air Force at the Tomb of the Unknown Soldier, the White House, the National Archives, the Pentagon, at formal banquets, and at Arlington National Cemetery.

There'd be no "going casual" here. Trainees work at their own pace to complete the program. They can take whatever time necessary to perfect the skills. Some graduate in three weeks; others take 10 or 12. I decided I could handle that. If I had nothing else, I had persistence, thanks to Sergeant Collier. I never dreamed that even that experience could turn out to be a blessing.

My first lesson as an honor guard trainee, or JEEP (junior experimental enlisted personnel), involved removing the buttons from my uniform jacket and pinning them back on so that the eagles would stay perfectly straight. Setting up one's locker was a lesson in itself. Our uniform buttons were to be lined up by size when we were not wearing our dress uniforms. At first it took me three hours to set up my locker to meet honor guard code. A piece of lint in a locker would cause the staff sergeant to upturn the contents, and the poor cadet would need to begin again.

Making one's bed was such a chore that many of the men chose to sleep under their beds at night so as not to have to remake them in the morning. While this behavior was not encouraged by the guard, it was commonplace.

Since I was a talkative individual, keeping quiet seemed next to impossible. Honor guards must be able to stand at attention without moving for long periods of time. Tourists try to make their lives difficult. Teenage girls stuff their phone numbers in guards' pockets or try to tickle them. Grannies ask questions, trying to get guards to talk. Little kids try to make them laugh. While there's always someone nearby who is supposed to be alert to any harassment a guard might be receiving, the honor guard is at the mercy of the annoyer until noticed.

Insects can be bothersome as well. Standing at attention in the White House Rose Garden can be hazardous, especially when roses are blooming. One day while I stood in formation, a honeybee landed on the brim of my hat. Out of the corner of my eye I watched it stroll from one side of my hat brim to the other. Then it dropped to the bridge of my nose and walked to the tip. I couldn't move. I couldn't twitch my nose, and, try as I might, I couldn't blow the creature away. Fortunately the offending bee chose to fly away rather than sting me. Even if it had stung me on the nose, I would not have been able to react.

Learning not to respond immediately to human or beast came difficult for me. My sanguine personality is eager to please when questioned. The day our instructor discussed the importance of remaining silent while in flight, he called us to attention, then said, "Talking in flight [on duty or at attention] is never, ever done. Johnsson, is that understood?"

"Yes, sir," I replied automatically.

"Airman Johnsson, you just did exactly what I told you not to do. You talked in flight. We're going to have to break this habit."

"Yes, sir!" The words barely escaped my lips when I realized what I'd done.

"You did it again. I want you to run to the stop sign down at the corner and tell the stop sign, loud enough so I can hear, that you will not talk while in flight again—four times. Now, run!"

I sped down the roadway and skidded to a stop at the corner a half mile away. Four times I gasped out the words "I will not talk in flight again," then ran back to where my unit remained at attention. I took my place in line, straightened my back, and stared straight ahead.

"Johnsson," the instructor asked, "what have you learned today?"

"Not to—" I groaned. I'd done it again! I couldn't believe myself.

"Johnsson," the instructor laughed good-naturedly, "you and your pledge to the stop sign will go down in honor guard history."

My courage flagged as each of my fellow trainees finished the program—three weeks, six weeks, seven weeks, 10 weeks—and I was still plodding through the requirements. I'd taken the finals a second time and failed to qualify. Somehow all the failures I'd endured in the past didn't equal the discouragement I felt this time.

I dragged myself back to my dormitory room that Friday night. My footsteps echoed down the long hallway. The majority of the JEEPs had left base for an evening on the town, so the dormitory was nearly empty. I could hear a local television newscaster reporting the evening news as I passed the doorway that led to the recreation lounge. *I'm not completely alone,* I thought. While I wished for a few minutes to myself, I hated the thought of being all alone. Once inside my room, I dropped into my desk chair and buried my head in my arms on the desktop. I wasn't about to put any wrinkles on my perfectly made bed—now, or later, at bedtime. I, like the others, chose to sleep under my bed rather than disturb a regulation-made bed.

Questions bombarded my brain. Would I be one of the JEEPs not to make it? Or would I make honor guard training history by being the first asked to quit trying? I heard a tap on my door. Before I could answer, it swung open, banging on the wall behind it. In came Reggie, a full honor guard who'd befriended me in secret and was giving me a lift to church each week. He befriended me in secret because there was an unwritten law preventing JEEPs and honor guards from fraternizing.

"What are you doing here?" I leaped to my feet in surprise.

"Grab your laundry bag and meet me in the laundry room in five minutes. Got that? Five minutes!" He gestured with his hand, then turned toward the door. Before closing it behind him, he leveled one last glare at me. "That's an order!"

I'd first met Reggie one evening when he'd seen me reading my Bible while I did my laundry. We learned that we were both Christians. He'd asked me if I were having any problems, and I'd told him I had only one—getting to church each week. I lacked personal transportation. Through a secretive routine that equaled the best of James Bond movies, he and his friend,

Coop, had taken me to church regularly. Obviously the news of my failure had reached them. They were the last people I wanted to see that evening.

Reluctantly I grabbed my laundry bag and trudged down the hall, like a prisoner walking to his execution. When I entered the laundry room, Reggie was sitting in one of the plastic chairs against the far wall. I started when the door slammed shut behind me. I turned to see Coop.

I shrugged. "So, here I am. Now what?"

"Hey," Reggie grinned, "where's that Johnsson spirit I hear everybody talking about?"

"Yeah, right," I grumbled.

Coop eased himself atop one of the washing machines. "Come on, we know you're discouraged, but you can't quit."

"I never said I was quitting," I mumbled like a surly teenager.

"Well, that's good," Reggie replied, "because I believe God has a purpose for you in the guard. Look how you got into the guard the first place. Talk about a miracle! You've overcome every stumbling block put in your way. You can do this, too."

"You're too close to reaching your goal to quit now," Coop added.

"All my friends are in the guard now. I'm all alone," I argued.

Coop snorted. "So? You sound like a spoiled 8-year-old."

"Sounds like you need a good shot of faith." Reggie rose to his feet. "We're here to pray with you, right here—right now!"

I stared up at the stern faces of my friends and knew this was no time to argue.

CHAPTER 5

"Stand by Me"

TWO WEEKS AFTER THE meeting in the laundry room with Reggie and Coop, I passed my final exams and officially became an honor guard. I'll never forget those guys. They were there for me. Their support gave me the courage to continue. And they put themselves on the line for me that night in the laundry room. If we'd been seen together, talking or praying, it was their necks as well as mine that were at stake. That's what friends do—put themselves on the line for one another.

I thank God that all my life, caring people have been there for me. My sister Linda defended me against all odds. My mother refused to take the advice of the school counselor to institutionalize me. Mrs. Shurlock as well as so many other of my elementary and secondary teachers stubbornly worked with me when it seemed impossible that I'd ever learn. My religion teacher showed me a world of need beyond Portland's street scene. Neighbors and church members saw more in me than I could ever see in myself.

My grandmother, Grazell Settles, made it a point to teach

me proper table etiquette. When her husband died after World War II, Grandma Settles obtained a degree in teaching from Prairie Bible College, then headed for Liberia as a missionary. Before her death in 1992, she'd started 13 girls' schools. She'd tell how young men would walk more than 100 miles to meet and marry one of her "girls." Today a former prime minister of Liberia is married to one of Grandma Settles' girls.

Whenever Grandma came home to America to raise money for her schools, she'd give large dinners at our home and invite some of the most important people in the area. In the process she became good friends with Billy and Ruth Graham. It was at one such fund-raising dinner that she predicted my birth. At the end of the meal Grandma Settles stood to give a toast and say thank you; then she added, "The Lord has told me that next year at this time, Zelma, you and Kenner will have a new baby boy."

My mother laughed. "That's impossible. Five children is quite enough." Old doctors and preachers in the Portland area today remember that dinner. They love to remind me of my grandmother's prediction.

Years later Grandma Settles told me that she'd shared only half of what God told her. The other half was that I would be a preacher, that I would carry on her mission of helping people and caring for those in need. "I'm not telling anyone until God brings it to pass."

At these dinners Grandma Settles would sit me down beside her. Whenever I reached for something without saying please or thank you or excuse me, she'd slap my hands and say, "Terry, I have a feeling that one day you will find yourself dining with the president of the United States. So you'd better learn to use proper manners now." At that time I never dreamed that her predictions would become a reality, that her lessons would take me all the way to the president's table.

We all need help from others, someone to keep us focused on what is important. My neighbors, my family, my Christian friends and church members, even the Boy Scouts and the Cub Scouts, guided me during my early years. When I needed help, all I had to do was ask and someone would be there for me.

To ask for help isn't always the easiest lesson to learn. I had a friend who needed help with an addiction, but he was too embarrassed to ask for it. When the subject came up, I reminded him that I was there for him, but he declined my offer. "If people were to find out what I'm really doing, they wouldn't like me anymore," he confessed. Because he didn't get help when he needed it, his problem grew, and before long everyone knew about his addiction. So many people would have been eager to help him if he had only been able to swallow his pride enough to ask.

One particular teacher in academy helped me when I needed help the most—Floyd Matula. When I was a teenager, my lifestyle spelled disaster. Parties, drugs, and alcohol threatened to destroy me as they had so many other teens. Floyd Matula made the difference for me.

Mr. Matula influenced me in two ways. First, he epitomized the word *gentleman*. Going into the cafeteria, he held the door open for others. He would help seat the women at the table before seating himself. If a girl approached the table, he would honor her by standing. I noticed these things. I also noticed that everyone liked him.

I decided to imitate Mr. Matula. Maybe, I reasoned, if I were nice like Mr. Matula, everyone would like me and my troubles would all go away. This decision changed my life. As my behavior improved, so did my popularity. I went from being one of the "underdogs" at school to being popular. I liked having my classmates say, "Terry is a nice guy." In time

I made up my mind that I wanted these qualities permanently in my life.

I spent hours talking with Mr. Matula. Between breaks in basketball practice, I'd slip away to his office to talk. I would voluntarily stay after school to spend time with him. As a result, he influenced me in a second way.

Mr. Matula accepted me as I was. He never prejudged me. By this time I'd started drinking and partying with my buddies. To make spending money, I sold shots of alcohol out of my school locker. Going to the shopping mall behind the school during school hours was not allowed, but I cut a hole in the school fence and charged the other students a dollar each to use it.

I thought I was a big shot. I determined to bury the injured 7-year-old boy inside me beneath tons of bravado and attitude. But my past continued to haunt me. In my senior year, when my SAT scores came back listing me as number 4 from the bottom out of 48 in my class, my teachers suggested that I take the test a second time. They thought something must have been wrong with the results. I knew there was nothing wrong with the test. The imperfections were in me. All the big noise and flashy attitude I could manifest couldn't hide the truth. I was incapable of learning.

Did Mr. Matula know what I was doing behind the scenes, what my life was like outside the classroom? Maybe, maybe not, but he must have had his suspicions. I do know he never condemned me. Whenever he confronted me about my problems, he'd say, "Terry, I trust you'll do the right thing," or "I know you know what is right, but the choice is always yours." As a result, I felt comfortable telling him about any problem on my mind.

Mr. Matula involved me in the speaking seminar program that he conducted. Each weekend he took students to speak in various churches in the Portland area. I'd given my first presentation while in grade school, a sermon on David and Goliath. I found that I enjoyed public speaking, and Mr. Matula picked up on that.

I did well until I tried to combine late-night partying with speaking engagements early the next morning. I'd go out drinking with my buddies, sometimes all night, then call my teacher in the morning and make excuses that I wasn't feeling well—which was all too true. Sometimes I'd say that I had to take my mother to church or that I was too tired, or that I had an obligation at my own church.

To my surprise, Mr. Matula wouldn't back down. "Terry," he'd say, "God really wants you to come with us today. If you don't, then your part in the program will not be filled. The other students are counting on you."

I knew that he realized that I'd been out partying. If I continued to say no, he'd bring the entire van of students to my house, knock on our door, and ask my mother if I could come out, because the other kids were counting on me. In time I stopped partying the night before I was to speak, because I didn't want to disappoint him. Eventually I stopped partying altogether—the influence of one caring teacher who refused to give up on me.

I know that if it were not for Mr. Matula having faith in me, I would never have finished academy. I probably would never have reached out for help on my own. His persistence made the difference. The man had a way of preaching to me through his lifestyle, rather than his words.

His quiet influence followed me to the White House. I believe that I became a favorite escort there because of the politeness I learned from him. While many of the honor guards had to learn the finer points of courtesy after joining the guard, mine came from years of being around Floyd Matula. Holding the door without being asked, looking after people's well-being, seating the generals' wives—the word got around. When they needed an escort for a special ceremony, I was often the first on the list called.

When I finished at Oakwood College and returned to Portland, I thanked Mr. Matula for all the time he had invested in me. He responded, "Terry, I could see that in your heart you wanted to do the right thing." For a man to admit he needs help is difficult. His machismo makes him believe he can do anything. He can handle life. He has all the answers. And if he also carries a heavy load of failure that he's trying to hide, to ask for help becomes a monumental struggle with his fabricated image.

I needed help. And thanks to Floyd Matula, I learned to turn to God first with my problems. I discovered that God waits eagerly and willingly to do for me, more than I could possibly ask. And in each difficulty, He was waiting for me to turn to Him.

You see, God is a perfect gentleman. He never forces Himself on us. He never forces us to be good, to be loving, to turn our lives around. But when we're ready, He's there to make that turnaround easy.

One day during my senior year of high school, I was in downtown Portland. I found a scrap of litter on the sidewalk. From my years of experience as a Boy Scout I picked it up, planning to toss it into the nearest trash bin. I glanced at it. It was a religious tract. On the cover it said, "God loves you."

Now, I'd been hearing "God loves you" my entire life. I'd been singing the children's song "Jesus Loves Me" since I was barely able to speak. But that day, at that moment in my life, the words spoke to me. I sat down on the nearest park bench and read the tract from cover to cover. The flyer said that God had a plan for my future. For regardless of Floyd Matula's faith in me, regardless of my English teacher's determination to help me through senior literature class, regardless of the city councilwoman's predictions, regardless of my mother's prayers and my grandmother's fretting, I knew the real Terry, the failure, the goof-up, the dummy. Could God really have something better in mind for me? On that park bench in downtown Portland I asked God for help. I was tired of trying to do it on my own. I couldn't play the macho game, the Joe-cool guy, any longer. When I told my best buddies of my decision, they scoffed.

"Terry, you can't leave us," one of them said. "You hang out with us. You party with us. What do you mean, you want God in your life? Aren't we enough?"

I looked at my friends and thought, *No, not anymore.* A short time later Barry Black, a Navy chaplain, held revival meetings in the area. I made up my mind during one of the meetings that my life needed to change. I would follow God.

After the meeting that night, my friends showed up at the church to take me to a party where I knew drugs and booze would flow. I told them I wasn't going, that I'd given my life to God.

"God?" My buddies laughed. "Come on, Terry. Stop kidding around. Besides, you gotta come with us. You're the life of the party."

I refused. They tried everything from mocking to reasoning to anger, but I didn't go.

Months later, while I was in the police academy, my mother called and told me that one of my buddies had been killed in a high-speed chase in a stolen car. The seat in the car most twisted and destroyed was the seat I usually occupied whenever we cruised together.

As for the third guy in our trio, Mike, he wasn't in the car that night—and for a good reason. I mentioned him earlier, in the chapter about dead ends. He's the one whose friends dropped acid in his drink at a party. He lives out his adult life, functioning as best he can, with the mind of a toddler.

God saw me that day in the park in downtown Portland, I have no doubt. And when I turned my face toward Him, He gathered me into His arms. He said, "Hello, son; I am here. I've been waiting so long for you."

"But, Father," I said, "I'm the kid they said was too stupid to learn. I'm the mental retard, remember?"

And the Lord just chuckled. "No problem, son, no problem. I've got you covered, covered by My grace."

I had no idea that God would take this kid who couldn't read and who stuttered whenever he became nervous, and make him a guard for the president of the United States.

Later, as God opened doors, revealing new and exciting pathways for my life, I remembered a story Grandma Settles told me when I was a child. She'd just returned home from Liberia for one of her fund-raising trips.

During an uprising against the government in that country, Grandma and the girls from one of the schools had to flee for their lives in the middle of the night. When morning dawned, Grandma found herself and the children far from civilization, huddled against the cold. Discouraged and hungry, she felt like giving up. Her heart wept for the cold and hungry children. In frustration she closed her eyes and cried out to God. "Lord," she said, "I really need Your help."

A tug on her sleeve caused her to open her eyes. Beside her stood a shivering little girl. "Mother Settles!" The child looked up in Grandma's face. "Didn't you tell us that God is always there for us? Didn't you tell us the story of how He helped Moses cross the Red Sea, and freed Joseph from prison, and helped Ruth find Boaz?"

My grandmother gathered the little girl into her arms. "Yes, child, yes. But unfortunately I'm not Joseph. I'm not Moses! And I'm not Ruth!"

"But isn't God the same God?" The child's simple answer silenced Grandma's questioning. At this point in the story, my grandmother would always pause. A broad smile would spread across her face. "Shame on me! Hadn't God already kept us safe through the long night, as we hid from the soldiers? It took a wee girl to remind me that God is still the same God."

Although I remembered Grandma's anecdotes and my mother's instruction, I had to discover this God for myself. I had to read for myself how God rescued Joseph from prison, how he preserved Daniel in a den of lions. I had to relive the story about how God delivered Daniel's friends from the raging fires without a whiff of smoke lingering on their clothing, or a hair on their heads singed. How He gave sight to those who were blind and life to those who were dead. I had to discover for myself that God does keep His promises. And He does it with style.

I didn't know as I scrubbed toilets for Sergeant Collier that I would become the first African-American honor guard from my home state of Oregon. I didn't realize at that time that I would also go down in president's honor guard history as the first guard with a disability, or that the guard would extend my tour of duty three times, or that I would serve the longest of any honor guard member up to that time. I received 12 badges, medals, and citations in less than four years, as well as a promotion to sergeant. I didn't know.

God will do incredible things with a willing but dyslexic young man declared unable to educate. Before I left military life to attend college, Grandma Settles' prophecy came true. I attended a special breakfast for the top honor guards at the White House, hosted by President Ronald Reagan.

But even Grandma Settles couldn't have imagined that I

would be privileged to meet every president since Richard Nixon, as well as to witness two inaugurations and two presidential funerals, those of Richard Nixon and Ronald Reagan. Yesterday—today—forever, God will always stand by me.

CHAPTER 6

IN HIS HONOR

THE DUTIES OF THOSE IN the honor guard vary—from presidential receptions to adding color at formal political functions to the president's inaugural ceremonies, and officiating at military funerals and funerals for heads of state. Honor guards also serve at the Tomb of the Unknown Soldier and as guides at the Pentagon.

When I passed the final test for the guard, I could choose between training for rifle duty or for funeral detail. I chose the latter. Hour after hour I practiced lugging caskets weighted with sandbags up the grassy slopes of Arlington Cemetery. I stood through long, tearful eulogies, learning not to respond emotionally. Finally, practice became reality. I could go through an entire funeral procession, a graveside service, and a 21-gun salute without a muscle twitch in my face.

I thought I'd conquered my feelings until our captain assigned our team to the Scobee funeral. The *Challenger* space shuttle tragedy had stunned America and had devastated the men in the Air Force. Commander Francis R. ("Dick") Scobee was one of us, a pilot who'd made it to the top in his field.

The morning the explosion occurred I peeled out of the recreation room at Fort Myer (I was in between funerals at Arlington) before the television commentator could complete his report. Despite the subzero weather, I tried to run off my emotions.

An unusual silence gripped our team members as we prepared for the funeral. None of the usual banter could be heard as we boarded the bus and drove to Arlington National Cemetery. My job that bitingly cold January morning was crowd control—in particular, corralling the members of the press. In their eagerness to get better camera shots, they often strayed beyond their cordoned area. My job was to chase them back. As we climbed the gray hillside that morning, I stayed near the rear of the casket to monitor the reporters and photographers.

The news personnel jostled one another for space behind the gold cord as the guards set the casket in place. As the mourners gathered about the grave, I felt grateful that I had something to do to keep my mind off the drawn faces of the commander's family.

The graveside ceremony progressed without penetrating my practiced military defense until Commander Scobee's brother lifted his trumpet to play "Taps." I could no longer choke back my tears when his notes quivered, then broke. I sniffed a few times, but nothing would stop the flow.

Fearful I'd made a spectacle of myself, I shot a glance at the other men in my unit. No one was concerned about my break in self-control, for tears streamed down their faces as well. A photographer chose that moment to lean across the restraining cord for a better shot of the trumpeter. *Bless you,* I thought, as I waved him back into place. The disturbance gave me a moment to regain my composure.

Riding back to the dormitory, I scolded myself. I

couldn't believe it. JEEPs might lose control of their emotions on an assignment, but not seasoned guards. Yet lose control I did, and on my first official assignment.

Then there came an assignment none of the other guards wanted. It was a $1,000-a-plate charity banquet; to an experienced guard it promised to be boring, but to me it sounded incredibly exciting, so I was overjoyed when I was chosen. My commander laughed at my eagerness and allowed me to fill the assignment.

When our bus arrived at the hotel in the District, we were surprised to see workers installing metal detectors at the doors. I asked a buddy if such tight security was used for every official function. My friend laughed. "Not usually," he said. "Now even the military brass and the members of Congress must be paranoid about terrorist attacks."

I shrugged it off. I had too many exciting things to consider. My gaze took in the mirrors, gold and crystal chandeliers, and the gleaming marble floors of the posh hotel. I wanted to recall every detail of the evening to share with my folks in Portland. Our sergeant in command led us to a side room where we changed into our dress uniforms.

When the sergeant assigned me my responsibility to open the front door to the banquet hall for the guests, I snapped off a crisp salute, smartly clicking my heels. He looked at me through half-closed eyes and shook his head. "Deliver me from JEEPs and their enthusiasm!" Proud to be wearing my crisp new uniform, I couldn't keep from grinning as I stood by the ornately carved doors.

I'd been at my post for less than 15 minutes when a colonel approached. I whipped off a salute and reached for the door handle.

The colonel eyed me curiously. "You like your job, don't you, son?"

"Yes, sir."

"Most guards don't enjoy this job."

"No, sir."

"And you do?"

"Yes, sir."

A strange little smile crossed the colonel's face. "Come with me, son. I have a different assignment for you tonight."

"Yes, sir!"

He took me to the front of the banquet hall, to the door on the right side of the podium. "I want you to stand here until I give you the signal to open the door. Got it?"

"Yes, sir." Standing inside the elegant banquet hall proved to be more entertaining than standing outside in the hallway. The waiters bustled about, adding last-minute details to the tables. The musicians clustered to one side of the dais, tuning up their instruments. And various military brass scurried through one door to another and to another, each intent on his or her own assignment. Reporters and photographers jostled one another for position. TV technicians ran wires from the microphones on the podium to the control room.

Before long the evening guests began to arrive. Members of Congress and their spouses strode into the ballroom. Decorated generals from all five branches of the armed forces, along with their spouses, were escorted to their tables. Important businesspeople arrived as well. My excitement grew as I realized how many of the guests I recognized from the television evening news.

However, I never took my attention too far from the colonel who would signal me to open the door. He'd trusted me with this post, and I didn't want to miss his signal. I would not pull a Gomer on such an important occasion.

With all the excitement, I considered who might be on the other side of the door when I opened it. Probably a four-star something or other, I imagined. When the colonel counted

"Three, two, one," and pointed at me, I grasped the brass door handle with my pristine white gloves, opened the door, clicked my heels together, and saluted.

My lower jaw dropped to the brass buttons on my chest. Entering through the opened doorway came, not a general or a representative or a senator, but the commander in chief, Ronald Reagan.

Cameras flashed. The band played "Hail to the Chief," and I froze in horror. *Oh, no, I've done it again!* I knew I was in deep trouble this time. As a new guard, I hadn't received my presidential clearance yet!

The president smiled at me and asked, "How are you doing tonight, airman? How are you doing?"

I'd boasted to my fellow guards about what I'd say if I ever met President Reagan in person. I wanted to ask him about his welfare plans, about the growing national debt, about the tax program for middle-income Americans, about the slashing of student loans. But there, face to face with my commander in chief, I blanked. All I could do was stutter.

The president turned to his aide. "I guess he's a little nervous," he said. The aide nodded and escorted Mr. Reagan to the platform. At the podium Reagan waved to his loyal followers until the music and applause faded. He told the audience he'd decided to attend the gala less than 45 minutes earlier. As he prepared to give his speech, he paused as if he had lost his train of thought, shook his head and grinned, then mumbled something about "that airman at the door."

Cameras flashed in my face and the press recorded the embarrassment lingering on my face.

It wasn't long after I entered the guard that an opening occurred for a year's stint as a narrator at the Tomb of the Unknown Soldier. I figured I had a good voice, and would try out for one of the five positions. Along with 49 other guards,

I applied. Again and again I practiced the script I'd been given. But on the day of the audition, when I saw so many others applying, the old terms popped back into my mind—*retarded, dummy, stupid.* Just before my turn came to audition I grew scared, really scared—so scared that I ran and hid like an 8-year-old boy.

I couldn't believe it, even as I cowered in my hiding place. I'd run away. The next day when the commander asked me why I missed my audition, I brushed him off with "I changed my mind."

That evening I picked up a book about reaching for your dreams, written by Robert Schuller. I read all night. In the morning I went to the commander and told him the entire story. As a result, the commander broke regulations to give me a special audition. My audition went so smoothly that the audition committee applauded when I finished. They appointed me to the only position to be filled at that time.

One day I saw an announcement on the bulletin board about an English class. I decided it was time for me to face my demons once and for all. I'd take the class. I would improve my reading.

I did fine until I came to the final test. I hated tests. While in school I would do anything I could to avoid taking tests. But this time I would not run.

As I stared at the typed sheets in front of me, I reminded myself that I'd already passed the difficult tests necessary for getting into the guard. I examined the test sheets before me. These were hardly more than vocabulary tests, similar to what I took in Mrs. Winter's English classes back in high school. One by one I finished the questions and gave the completed form to the instructor.

Painfully I watched as the red pen highlighted the wrong answers. When the instructor finished, she looked across the desk at me. "Man, your tutor must have been outstanding."

"Excuse me? What tutor?"

"The one who helped you with your dyslexia. Must have been a genius."

I scowled. "Dyslexia? What dyslexia?"

"Your parents must have spent a bundle on you."

"I-I-I don't know what you're talking about. My parents never had that kind of money."

She ignored my remarks. "Airman Johnsson, you just might be the first person with a disability ever to be in the president's honor guard."

I stared at her in confusion.

She removed her glasses. "Don't you know that you have dyslexia in the third degree? How in the world did you pass your Air Force admissions tests, let alone the psychological and military aptitude tests—there's no way!"

"I have what?" I still wasn't comprehending.

"Do you have trouble reading and spelling?"

I remembered Mrs. Pennyworth's classes and stiffened. "Yes, ma'am."

"That's because you have dyslexia, a reading disorder." She went on to explain that people with dyslexia often see letters backwards. Sometimes the letters dance around on the page. I listened in amazement. How did she know?

"Often such students are considered underachievers because their brains can't process the words correctly. You must have had some of the best tutors around. For a person of your degree of dyslexia, you've reached a point where it is almost undetectable." She studied my folder once again.

I mentally jogged through my grade school years and academy. "As far as I know, I've never had a tutor in my entire life." My brother's girlfriend, Jennifer, had once helped me with spelling. But that was all I could bring to mind.

The woman chuckled and shook her head. "You just don't remember. There is no way in the world you could have passed the Air Force exams without at least two years of college classwork."

I thought for a moment. "My parents have been praying about my lack of reading skills for years. I know that God has helped me with my reading problem. Otherwise, I didn't even know I had this dyslexia thing."

The examiner's eyes glazed over at the mention of God, but I continued. "In high school I had an English teacher, Mrs. Winters, who worked with me after class. She had me read a chapter of the Bible aloud until I could read it perfectly. And in third grade, Mrs.—"

"No, no, no! I don't believe it! There must be some record here of a specially trained tutor or coach."

"Mrs. Winters' granddaughter helped me sometimes—"

"No, that wouldn't do it either. Your progress would have taken years of intensified training, costing thousands of dollars."

"Thousands of dollars?" I laughed. "My parents never had that much money in their entire lives. It had to be the Bible."

The examiner shook her head. "The Bible?"

"Let me tell you about myself." I smiled and relaxed a little. "When I was in first and second grade . . ." I told her about Mrs. Pennyworth, my elementary and secondary experience, and about my military career thus far. "So you see, considering all He's done for me, I'm not surprised to learn that God and His Word have been my tutors all along. By the way, could my problem—this dyslexia—have affected other areas of my life as well?"

"Absolutely!"

As I returned to my dormitory room, everything began to make sense. Dyslexia! Of course, it would affect my reading as a kid, my marching, and several other problems I'd been facing in the military. *Imagine,* I thought, *God helped me overcome a disability I didn't even know I had.*

Here I was on a new adventure, one that far surpassed any dream I might have had for my life. Now that my problem had been identified, what could go wrong? It would be smooth riding the rest of the way.

However, a native Northwesterner knows that every road has its potholes. The pothole in my road to the honor guard took the form of Wes Conners (not his real name), a guardsman who hated me from the first time we met.

Throughout my life I'd come up against people who disliked me, either because of my dyslexia or my color, so Wes's animosity was nothing new. When people treated me like this, I set out to change their minds.

Edwin Markham wrote a poem called "Outwitted."

> He drew a circle that shut me out—
> Heretic, rebel, a thing to flout.
> But love and I had the wit to win:
> We drew a circle that took him in!

I would simply win Wes over by including him in my circle of love. With most people, my method of fighting prejudice with kindness worked, but not with Wes Conners. He hated my skin color. He hated my personality. He hated my positive attitude. But most of all, he hated my faith in God.

One evening each week a group of trainees would meet to study the Bible and pray together. Far from home for the first time, I'd learned early in my military experience that I needed the prayers and encouragement of my friends. Since I wasn't the only airman who felt this need, we banded together for support.

Our prayer circle irritated Wes. And being a loudmouth and

a self-proclaimed atheist, he let his opinions be known. Inasmuch as I was the de facto leader of the prayer group, he aimed his barbs at the preacher boy—me. Every opportunity he found to mock, to poke fun at me or my religion, he used it. He considered men who believed in God to be wimps or pantywaists. He claimed they couldn't stand on their own two feet. His turns occurred most often when we were on assignment.

At times I wanted to flatten him, to show him that my bulk was far from weak. I fantasized about the surprised look I'd see on his face when I sent him flying onto his backside. *Just once,* I fantasized. *Just once!*

Yet I knew slugging Wes Conners was not an option for me, not because Wes was so tough, but because everyone knew I claimed to be a Christian. And trouncing one's enemies is not part of the Christian code.

In my short time in the honor guard to this point, I had discovered that we often spent several hours on the bus, riding to and from assignments. To pass that time, I packed a couple paperback books or a New Testament to read. Sometimes I'd bring along extra reading material for other guys to borrow as well.

One humid midsummer morning our entire unit headed for the White House for a flag ceremony. Canada's prime minister Brian Mulroney and his wife were visiting the Reagans. During the morning's full-uniform inspection we'd been warned to bring along our smelling salts. It would be a long ceremony, in stifling temperatures. We'd be standing at attention in the sun—a perfect day to "flake."

Flaking, or passing out while at attention before the president of the United States or some other high political personage, brings shame and embarrassment to your entire branch of the military. While friendly banter flowed between the five branches—the Air Force, the Army, the Navy, the Marines, and the Coast Guard—each branch claimed to be tougher and better trained than the others. No one wanted to appear weak or to fail their branch. And a flake was considered the worst of transgressions for a guard. Pictures of any guard who fainted could end up on the cover of the Washington *Post* or *Times*. I felt along the rim of my hat for the tiny flask of ammonia I hoped I'd never need.

Wes Conners began taunting me before we boarded the honor guard bus that morning. "So, holy boy, who's gonna flake today?" he asked. He glanced at the Bible in my hand. "I see you brought along your magic book, Johnsson."

I ignored his jibes, but he continued: "You know, your God is nothing more than a spook, a figment of your imagination."

I turned my back, refusing to give him the satisfaction of an answer. The guardsman behind me took on my cause. "Hey, Wes, knock it off, will ya? Leave Johnsson alone."

Wes snarled at him out of the corner of his mouth. "Figures, a wimp like Johnsson needs someone else to fight his battles."

Another guardsman overheard Wes's jibes. "Cut it out, Wes. You're just spoiling for a fight."

Wes snorted as he climbed onto the bus. "Hmmph! No threat from that pantywaist."

When I boarded, I noted that Wes had chosen to sit in the back. I decided to choose a seat as far from him as possible.

"Good choice, Johnsson," Wes shouted. "If you came back here, you might have to stand up for something." He laughed at his own joke. The guards around him didn't.

"One of these times you're going to get Johnsson mad enough to fight," the man on Wes's right warned.

"Ho, ho! Right! Holy boy may fight me and get his halo bent." Wes hooted with laughter.

I fought the anger building inside of me and determinedly stared out the bus window. I swiped at the sweat dripping down the sides of my face. The air-conditioning on the bus couldn't keep pace with the heat and humidity of the day, nor could it cool the fury rising inside of me.

"Hey, holy boy, why don't you ask your God to give us some shade out there today? As if He could."

"Give it a break, Wes," someone called out.

Conners wouldn't be silenced. "Pack your clothes, holy boy; you're leaving today. You're gonna flake."

I gripped the seatback in front of me and rose partway. "Wes, that's enough!"

"Oh, big threat!" Wes mimicked me in a high childish voice.

"You know, Wes," I pointed my finger at him, "you could flake, you know."

"Me?" the guardsman laughed. "Hey, I've been a guard for a long time. I've had worse assignments than this! You'll fall out long before I will." He preened before the attention of the rest of the guards. "Why, even God Himself couldn't make me fall out!"

Silence descended on the busload of guards. A sergeant seated in the front of the bus turned around. "OK, Conners, you're pushing it too far."

Wes blinked his eyes in innocence. "Hey, Sarge! What can I say? It's true. Even Johnsson's God couldn't make me flake!"

A chill skittered up my spine. I shook my head at Wes. "Conners, you should never have said that."

Wes threw back his head and laughed. "Like I'm really scared."

We arrived at the White House and donned our dress uniforms. Locating the Wyoming state flag, the one assigned for me to carry, I fell into line. A marine behind me jabbed me in the back and joked, "Good day for a flake, eh, flyboy?"

"Not on your life, jarhead," I retorted.

Out front on the lawn of the White House portico presidential aides, White House staff, the press, and television crews, about 400 in all, gathered. A tangle of cords and microphones trailed up to the lectern that had been placed in the center of the first landing. The honor guards, each carrying a state flag, would form the colorful backdrop for the ceremony honoring Prime Minister Mulroney and his wife.

On cue, we marched into place up the stairs of the portico and onto the balcony behind the dais. Five, 10, 15 minutes passed. As we stood at attention, the sun bore down on our heads. Our polyester/woolen uniforms itched. Sweat oozed down our backs and necks. More time passed. The president and the prime minister were running far behind their schedule. But who's going to interrupt the president of the United States and our closest ally? More time passed. I tried to focus my thoughts on anything but the intolerable conditions I had to endure.

I'd been giving a lot of thought to my future after I left the honor guard. Discovering that my learning problems had a name, dyslexia, and was not a sign of mental retardation befuddled my thought process. Maybe college, a four-year program, would be nice. And maybe the childhood dream of becoming a preacher just might be possible after all. My mind expanded with the possibilities.

I snapped alert as the first strains of "Hail to the Chief" filled the sultry air. The doors swung open, and the president and Mulroney walked out into the sunlight. Mrs. Reagan and Mrs. Mulroney followed. Cameras flashed with the usual cacophony of whirs and clicks. The president stepped up to the podium and began speaking. The longer he talked, the hotter the sun became. Reagan showed no signs of reaching the end of his prepared message. I took long, slow, and deep breaths and thought cool thoughts—climbing snow-covered Mount Hood, a dip in the Pacific Ocean at Cannon Beach, swimming in the Columbia River . . .

Out of the corner of my eye I saw a movement on the opposite side of the president. A flag along the balcony wavered. What followed broke up the entire ceremony. The loud crack of the flagpole hitting the concrete sounded like a gunshot, causing President Reagan to jump. Secret service men reached inside their jackets for their guns, at the same time scanning the audience for the would-be assassin.

Wes had wobbled back and forth, then collapsed. His flag rolled down several steps. The sergeant behind Wes snatched the vial from his own hat rim and shoved it under Wes's nose.

Electrified into action by the sudden movement, the press located the source of the disturbance and had a riotous field day recording for posterity the "flaking" of the guardsman. Also recorded forever was the small stream of water that trickled down the steps from where Wes sat, bewildered and dismayed. He'd wet his pants—a final coup de grâce to what went down in Air Force honor guard history as the worst "flaking" ever recorded.

On the bus trip back to base that night Wes didn't say much. Neither did the other guards. But at our Monday night prayer time the size of our group doubled. I guess the men didn't want to take any chances with our God. Much later Wes and I became friends.

So many times I had been tempted to solve my problem with Wes by myself. In the end God's method worked better than anything I could have imagined.

CHAPTER 7

LEARNING TO CARE

I HAD NEVER EXPERIENCED such loneliness as I felt during my time in the military. I'd never before been so far from home and from the ever-present support of my family and friends. Suddenly my close-knit family wasn't there for me, except by telephone. I couldn't sit around the kitchen table with my mom and dad and spill out my heart over a glass of milk and a slice of sweet potato pie.

Hearing their voices over the phone brought on an ache so deep within me that I couldn't shake it off when I hung up. My loneliness deepened when I received the fateful call from my girl back home, the call that ended a longstanding relationship. It had come soon after I was forced to "go casual."

I had first met Mia when I was 5 years old. Our fathers worked together, and our mothers attended a morning club, so our families carpooled four days a week. Mia and I hated each other. Our earliest memories were of riding in the back seat of the car and fighting. If I touched her arm she would say I had boy germs, which would make me touch her arm all the more. Our quarreling didn't end when we reached school. The teacher would make us sit in chairs to stop the fighting.

For the next two years we were determined enemies. When Mia transferred to a parochial school in the area, we lost touch with one another.

After the incident in second grade with Mrs. Pennyworth, my mother transferred me to a Christian school, which I attended until the sixth grade. At that time my folks transferred me to another church-run school, Portland Adventist Elementary.

My courage flagged that first morning as I climbed aboard the school bus to head for my new school. My only comfort was that my niece Shannon would be riding on the same bus. She and I were the last kids picked up from the east side. When she boarded the bus, she took the first available seat, leaving me to go all the way to the back of the bus to find a place to sit. Worse yet, the only seat available was next to a girl! I could hardly think of anything worse than to be forced to sit by a girl. The girl took one look at me, frowned, and moved as far from me as she possibly could.

We didn't speak the entire bus trip. As we rode I kept looking at her through the corner of my eye. Occasionally I would catch her doing the same with me. During recess that morning she came up to me and said, "I thought that was you. You don't remember me, but my name is Mia." My mouth dropped open, and I stared unabashedly as she walked away from me. I hadn't seen her since preschool. Mia was by far the most beautiful girl I'd ever seen, but I had no intention of letting her know that at that time.

Nothing else changed between us. We began fighting again. We argued about everything. She was my worst enemy the entire school year! Whenever we had our biggest fights, people would tell us that it was a sign that we really liked each other. This forced us to put on a dramatic show of how much we disliked each other. Mostly we'd yell and call each other names. At times Mr. Williams, the bus driver, would pull over and make one of us sit in front of the bus and the other in the back.

Our relationship changed the night my cousin Yolanda invited all my friends from the neighborhood and from school to my birthday party. Mia sat beside me all evening. We had the greatest time together. We laughed and talked as if we were old friends. But at the end of the evening I still didn't trust her. I kept waiting to feel her first sarcastic jab. It never came.

During the party my friend Sean invited me to go roller skating with him and his friends the next evening. Mia made certain I knew she would also be attending. When I got to the rink, I saw her from afar. And that's the way it stayed all evening until the last skate. My cousin Robin grabbed Mia by the hand and brought her to me. "Terry, skate with Mia." Robin thrust Mia's hand into mine and left us standing there looking at each other. By the end of the skate we were crazy about each other.

Mia and I dated for more than four years until I went into the military. When she learned that I'd enlisted and would be leaving home almost immediately, she cried. The night before I left for Texas we discussed our situation and decided to wait to marry until after I'd completed my military training. The separation turned out to be more than our relationship could take. I never felt so empty and alone as I did the night I hung up the phone from talking with her. She cried and I cried until there was nothing to say but goodbye.

Knowing I had to go back to a less-than-friendly environment made it all the more difficult. With every abusive word or deed that my training instructor heaped upon me I became lonelier still. Yet I longed to be alone, to think about my situation. When the other guys went to the base recreation hall, I hosted major pity parties in my room, at which I was the only guest. The temptation to quit, to give it all up, to go home, constantly teased the corners of my consciousness. At the police academy I felt more out of place and lonelier than before, if possible. I wanted to share my anxieties, but to whom could I go? My buddies? They were gung ho for combat training. That's why they had signed up for the academy in the first place. My training instructor? Hardly.

When I was forced to go casual, my isolation became almost overwhelming. The other cadets had moved on to their assignments. So whatever friendships I might have been forming ceased. As my loneliness built, I blamed others. It was everyone else's fault, not mine. And eventually I blamed God. I cried out in my frustration, "Why are You punishing me? It's not fair!"

At the time, I couldn't understand anything but my own misery. I couldn't see that God had a plan for me and that I needed to learn to wait on Him. But with my mother and the base chaplain telling me to stick it out, I managed to hold on through the lonely times.

One of the loneliest times came the first year when I transferred to the president's honor guard in Washington. Because of the holiday galas in the nation's capital, the weeks between Thanksgiving and New Year's Eve were the busiest for the honor guard. As a result, half the guards had a Thanksgiving furlough, and the other half had Christmas.

Distance and cost prohibited me from going home, which meant that I'd spend both Thanksgiving and Christmas alone—3,000 miles from my family. The other guards, with only one of the holidays with their families, were no happier than I. Wherever I went I heard grumbling and complaining about the situation. That's when I remembered Floyd Matula, my academy religion teacher. Mr. Matula had a policy that he shared with me—"When you're feeling bad, find someone who has bigger problems to help, and you'll forget your own."

One summer I got a job taking surveys to identify the most critical needs of the residents in the poorest neighborhoods of Portland. To me the whole thing was a big joke—easy money. I thought the people were just lazy and didn't want to work. I'd heard stories of swindlers pretending to need food and money. I'd heard about welfare fraud. I remembered how Peter, a neighbor of ours, had defrauded the welfare system. I had no sympathy for people who lived only to con others.

My biggest on-the-job concern was to hurry and finish the report at the end of the day so I could go home. I remember knocking on doors, hoping no one would answer; seeing people on porches and purposely walking by without stopping—something I regret today.

Because of my summer employment I signed up for an high school class called Outreach, an easy A. The instructor, Mr. Matula, had heard about my summer job and asked me to be his assistant. After people asked for help, Matula and I would go to their homes to speak with them. He would remind me that before entering a person's home, I should put away any judgmental attitude and open my heart to that person. "Ask God to help you see Him in everyone." I tried it. I was shocked at what I saw—abused wives who had barely enough money to put a supper of Campbell's soup and day-old bread on the table; elderly people who spent all their Social Security checks for medicine, leaving nothing for food or to heat their meager rooms. The more I listened, the softer my heart became. I'd prayed that God would soften my heart, and He did. We found elderly people who needed their homes painted. Some needed groceries; others couldn't do the yardwork and upkeep. Some needed warm clothing.

AIM HIGH

erry was 6 years old and
tending public school
hen it was determined
at he had a learning
sability.

Terry Johnsson is the sergeant in charge of the honor guard at Arlington National Cemetery.

The first honor guard team Terry was in charge of.

Preparing for the funeral of Francis R. Scobee, Air Force commander of the Space Shuttle *Challenger*, at Arlington National Cemetery. (Terry is in the front right.)

Andrews Air Force Base. Standing on the runway, waiting for *Air Force One* to come in with the president. (Terry is back right.)

On the way to a winter White House ceremony.

Typical day of greeting the president when he returns from a trip. (Terry is to the left, behind President Reagan.)

. dignitary visit for the prime minister of India at Andrews Air Force Base.
Terry is the fourth honor guard from the right.)

t the Tomb of the
nknown Soldier for
full honor Air Force
reath-laying ceremony.
Terry is the sergeant in
harge.)

Another wreath-laying ceremony. (Terry is on the honor guard team.)

Annual White House group photo. This photo of the full Air Force honor guard is presented to the president.

State and territory flags (actual setup when the honor guard is posting the flags on the White House lawn). Honor guards from all branches of the military: Army, Navy, Marines, Air Force, Coast Guard. (Terry is second to the left.)

A typical setting up of the flags for a full honor White House ceremony on the White House grounds. Thousands of onlookers have begun to line up on the other side of fence.

Full honor arrival ceremony for the Japanese minister of defense at the Pentagon. (Terry is the fifth man from the right. At the far left is Frank Carlucci, U.S. secretary of defense.)

Terry was one of the handpicked Air Force honor guard to be part of Mikhail Gorbachev's first visit to United States.

Terry's very first ceremony at the White House. The ceremony is for the prime minister of Canada.

Above: Marching on the White House grounds to prepare for a full honor ceremony.

Terry doing narration at the White House, introducing one of the many dignitaries who visit each year.

Above: President Reagan's farewell in an Air Force hangar at Andrews Air Force Base.

his photo, taken at the inaguration of George Bush, was
gift to the handpicked Air Force honor guard, the 20
ho were ushers.

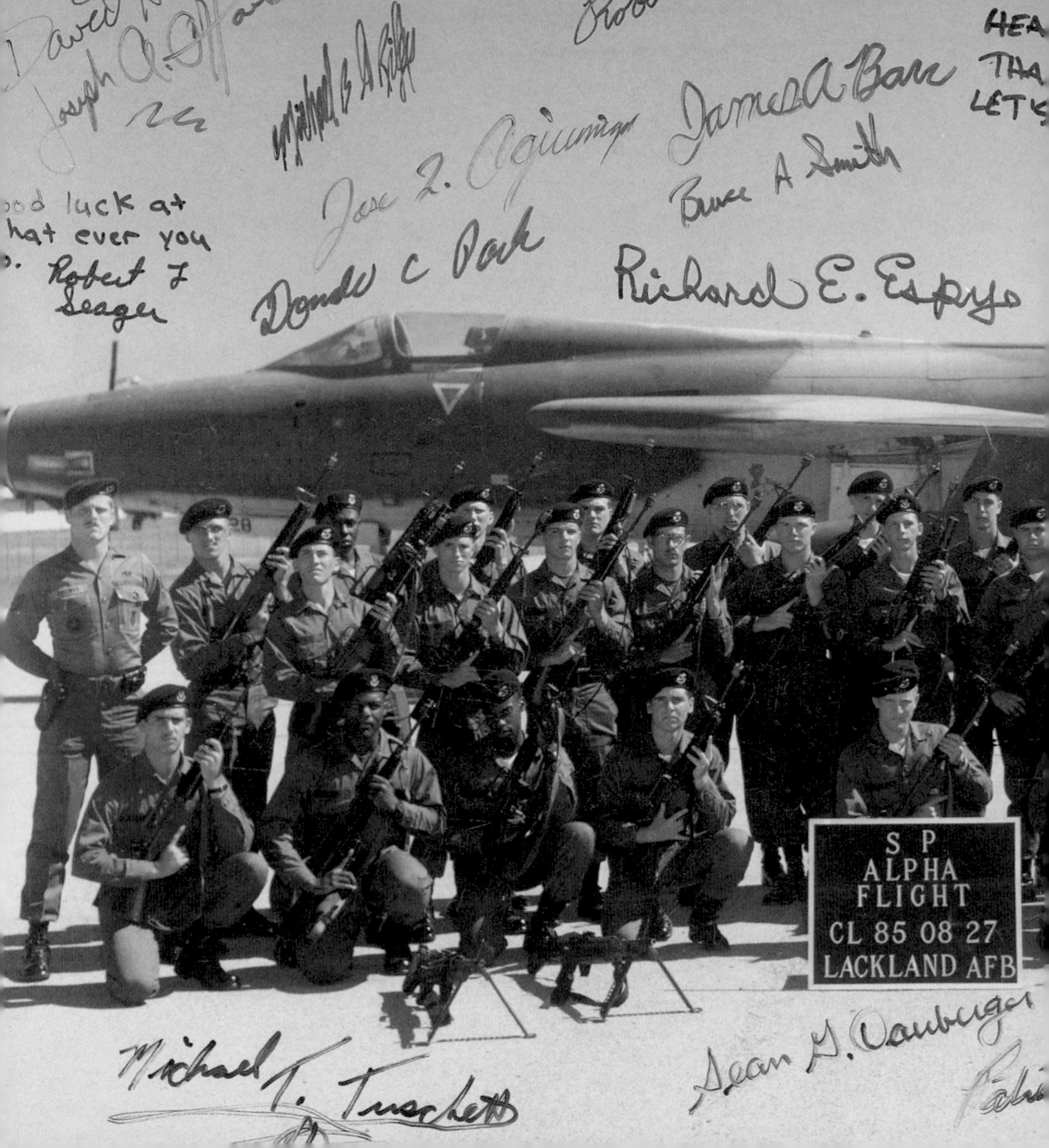
Robert A Lambert
James A Barr
Bruce A Smith
ood luck at
hat ever you
Robert J
Seager
S P
ALPHA
FLIGHT
CL 85 08 27
LACKLAND AFB

Terry's Air Force Police Academy graduation photo (back row, third from left).

Terry receiving the Air Force Award of Excellence of Washington, D.C., from Colonel Welsh.

Terry receiving his diploma upon graduating from noncommissioned officer school.

First-ever speaking engagement at the Rockville church in Portland, Oregon.

While Terry was in the military, Robert Schuller was one of the authors he read who inspired him to go to college.

Presidents Terry served under: Ronald Reagan (not pictured), George Bush (left), and Bill Clinton (below).

This photo of George W. Bush was a gift from the White House to Terry Johnsson.

AIM HIGH

Terry at Oakwood College, freshman year, after leaving the military.

Terry speaking at an evangelistic meeting in Ghana, West Africa. At this writing, Terry has spoken in more than 60 countries.

I knocked on one door, and a little girl answered. She invited us in. "Mommy's waiting for you. Did you bring food? We don't have any food here in the house."

The child invited us to sit down while she told her mother we were there. As I looked around the room, I had the biggest shock of my life. On the mantel I saw a photograph of Frank (not his real name), one of my classmates. That this mother was struggling, not having enough food to feed her kids, and that one of her kids went to school with me every day seemed impossible to believe. I'd barely recovered when the mother entered the room, followed by Frank.

As she spoke with Mr. Matula about getting some clothes for Frank, I could see the hurt and embarrassment in Frank's eyes. I could tell he was thinking that I'd go back to school and tell everyone about the poverty conditions I'd seen in his home. Before I left the house, I took Frank aside and said, "Frank, you have nothing to be ashamed of. We all go through hard times."

At graduation everyone was buying good-looking outfits for the event. I knew Frank didn't stand a chance of having a new suit, so a friend of mine, Terry Gish, and I bought Frank an outfit. Incredibly, my friend shared the expense without ever knowing who the recipient was. Today Frank is quite well off, making good money in the computer industry. And to this day he gives me a hug every time he sees me, and thanks me for not telling the other kids.

It was easy to condemn suffering people when I wasn't around them. From my comfortable home or school, surrounded by my family, I never came across a truly hurting person. For the first time, I realized that I couldn't erase the pain by turning off the television or by switching channels. These were real people who had families, people with feelings, hunger pangs, who needed clothing and medicine and toothpaste. And their hurt went on day after day, night after night. Coming in direct contact with pain, seeing the people through Another's eyes, God's eyes, changed me.

That same school year a sister of mine, who lived in Los Angeles, died. With limited funds, my parents had to choose between flying from Portland to California to settle my sister's estate or paying my school tuition. The choice was obvious. I'd have to leave school. But the principal and a few other staff members had compassion on me and arranged for me to stay in school so that I could graduate with my class.

In the honor guard, away from home the first Christmas after my sister's death, intensified my loneliness. But the other guards were affected too. Boredom between assignments caused tempers to flare; our nerves chafed from the frustration of being among strangers and so far from our loved ones. I knew that I, for one, needed a change of attitude.

Frustrated, I headed for bed early one night. There, as I pouted over my situation alone in the darkness, I remembered Mr. Matula's words: "There is always someone worse off than you and who could use a little help." During the holidays volunteer agencies need all the help they can get.

H'mmm, I thought, *if anyone needs to get their thoughts off themselves it's us.* The next morning I went to see the commander. "Sir, I'm going stir-crazy. Do you know of any agencies that feed the homeless and that might need some help during the holidays?"

Later Sergeant Washington suggested I call Georgetown University Hospital. "I read in the paper that the hospital feeds the senior citizens of the community every Thanksgiving," he said.

I contacted the hospital and they accepted my offer to help; possibly I could bring a few friends along as well. After I hung up the phone, I posted a sign on the dormitory bulletin board. "Instead of griping about our problems, why not help someone else? Sign up to help feed the senior citizens of Georgetown on Thanksgiving Day."

As we boarded the bus for the hospital on Thanksgiving morning, I checked off the names of those who'd signed up. I'd expected 10 or 12 volunteers, but 30 came!

My friends and I peeled, whipped, beat, chopped, pureed, and grated until our fingers hurt, but we had fun. We were too busy to miss being home. Best of all, we mingled with the guests, helping seat them and serve them, and just being friendly. After we had dried the last dish and scoured the last scorched pan, the members of the hospital staff thanked us for our help. "I don't know how we could have ever done this without you guys," the supervisor of the event told us.

On the way back to the base several of the guards thanked me for arranging the day's activity. "I've never been so beat in all my life," one guard admitted. "I may never be able to look another potato in the eye again. Thanks for inviting me to go along."

Another guard added, "Before today, I never realized how neat old people can be. I met a woman who's related to Pocahontas. Imagine that—Pocahontas."

That evening, as the winter sun disappeared behind the Virginia hills, 30 Air Force guards returned to base, exhausted but content. It had truly been a happy Thanksgiving.

That night as I finished my shower, one of the worst complainers in our unit asked, "Hey, Johnsson, what are we doing for Christmas?" I expected to see a sneer, but instead his face glowed with excitement.

As Christmas approached, I found a number of community agencies that could use our help. The days sped by as busloads of guards traveled all over the D.C. area, collecting food and toys for families in need. The public couldn't believe what they saw. The president's honor guards had never before involved themselves in the local community and its needs.

Soon after the first of the year Sergeant Washington called me into his office to meet the honor guard commander. I shook inside as I entered the office. What had I done wrong this time?

The commander greeted me with "Young man, I want to shake your hand. You have brought the United States Air Force Honor Guard more good PR in four weeks than most guards contribute throughout their entire service in the unit."

Speechless, I grinned, and nodded a thank-you.

"I have received a flood of letters from the Georgetown University Hospital personnel, from the Washington Catholic Diocese, from military brass, and even the mayor's office, commending you for your volunteer work here in the capital. You've begun a good thing for the guard. I hope you'll keep it going."

"Yes, sir." What I'd done had been as much for my own happiness as it had been for the people we had helped.

After the holidays we started a sack lunch program for the homeless in Washington; we involved the guard in the Toys for Tots program; we continued helping prepare and serve food to seniors; and we began visiting the Old Soldiers' Home. Every two weeks we'd visit the retirement center to get acquainted, listen to the residents' stories, and be their friends.

One time the unit commander assigned one of the crustiest of sergeants to drive the van that would take us to Washington's Children's Hospital, where we would hand out teddy bears to the children in the cancer ward. This sergeant did not want to go. He pledged he would sit in the van.

The children loved our uniforms and shiny medals. They'd run up to us, grab us, and hug us. Because they had so much love to give, we couldn't get away. Well, the sergeant waiting outside became impatient enough to come in to see what was taking so long. When he did, one little 8-year-old girl spied him and dashed into his startled arms. "Thank you. Thank you for coming to see us," she squealed with delight, wrapping her arms tightly around his neck. "I love you."

Taken aback by the child, the sergeant started to cry. He picked up the girl, sat down with her on his lap, and talked with her. When it was time to leave, he didn't want to go. When I left the guard, the sergeant took over the program. He made sure that the teddy bears for the children program continued. He developed one of the most positive attitudes ever in the president's honor guard. Not only did he change, but so did the entire unit. We became known as one of the most compassionate units in the honor guard.

A few years ago our unit received the Presidential Unit Citation Award, the highest award a unit can receive, largely because of the humanitarian efforts carried out for the community—all because of loneliness. God used each of the men's loneliness to teach us compassion.

Now that I'm not in the military, I still have times when I feel lonely. Somehow the excitement of a visit to Disney World or a speaking engagement in Hawaii dims when I've no one with whom to share the experience. But God knows that too. And in His perfect time He will fulfill that need in me.

For three years I dated a young woman while I attended Oakwood College in Alabama. But my busy speaking schedule kept us apart too often. We broke up just before graduation. My heart was crushed. I'd dated other girls during my military stint, but I had never been as serious about any of them. I believed she'd be the perfect minister's wife. The loneliness settled in once again. I thought, *It seems so easy. It seems as if God has just the right person for other people at just the right time. Why can't He do the same for me?*

Some years later I talked with my mother about being single and, as a result, often lonely. She told me to stop complaining. "Terry, don't you realize it would have been impossible for you to do all you've done if you had had the responsibilities of a wife and family? God is using your singleness to bless you." I didn't like what I was hearing, but I knew she was right.

"Think about it. Since leaving the military, you've completed college, earning two degrees. Do you know how many young men have to defer those dreams because of family obligations? You've traveled around the world to more than 60 countries, speaking to thousands of people for God. Could you have done that with the responsibility of a wife and young children?

"Terry, you finished graduate school in record time, and you're still under 30. God has used your aloneness to bring glory to His name."

Half serious, I asked, "Are you saying God can't use a person if he's married?"

"Of course not. God can use you in any circumstance. But you've been like the apostle Paul. It's been easier for you to do God's work because the only person you're accountable to is God. And remember, being alone doesn't mean you have to be lonely. Look at your sister Brenda. She enjoys her solitude."

"Yeah," I laughed, "one day I found her sitting in the middle of her living room floor in her Beverly Hills apartment, reading three books at the same time. Can you imagine?"

"Remember, Terry, before you can enjoy other people, you must start by enjoying your own company."

I was speaking in a very large city one day. At the end of my presentation my host told me there was a man waiting near the side door who wished to speak with me. I went to meet the man. He said, "I'm a chauffeur. My boss wishes to have lunch with you. She feels she has lots in common with you."

I lifted my eyebrows in surprise. How in the world could a

wealthy woman who had her own chauffeur-driven limousine have anything in common with me? "That would be fine," I assured him.

"Bring along your host as well. He knows where madam lives."

Now, I have been a guest in several beautiful homes in my lifetime, especially in the Washington, D.C., area. Senators, representatives, businesspersons—incredible homes. But this woman's estate had to be the grandest. A butler met us at the door, escorted us into the family room, and invited us to be seated. A sweet elderly woman entered the room and introduced herself. She wasted little time getting to her story.

She'd been living in a nursing home with very few friends. In 10 years not one family member had come to visit her. As the years passed, she lost her faith in God. She became grouchy and bitter. One day a large, smiling Black woman, one of the nurse's aides, entered her room and said, "It's a beautiful day."

"I don't see anything beautiful about it," she answered.

The woman went on. "We exchanged this same greeting day after day, year after year. No matter how sorry I felt for myself, this nurse's aide wouldn't give up on me. She was my friend."

I smiled, thinking of all the women in the Sharon church back in Portland that would fit that picture.

The woman continued. "One day the nurse asked me what hobbies I had enjoyed when I was younger. I thought for a time, then told her that I loved to paint. I'd painted as a child and all the way through college. When I got married and my children came, I stopped painting."

A couple weeks later the aide brought the older woman a lovely set of watercolors. She asked the older woman to paint something. "My friend really seemed to enjoy my work," the woman said. "Then the other nurses asked for my paintings. Even the director of the nursing home asked me to do a couple for his office. So at that very old age I began a career of painting.

"One day my friend said there was a woman who had just arrived at the home who would like to see me. This woman wrote poetry, some of the most beautiful poetry I'd ever read.

"The nurse's aide suggested that we get together and produce a line of greeting cards—this woman's poetry and my art. That's what started the whole thing. Requests came from all over, including from the state governor. We were offered a very large sum of money for our creations, more than I'd ever seen in my entire life."

The woman handed me several samples of her designs. "As a result, I became a very wealthy woman very late in life. Imagine going from life in a nursing home, with no friends and no family, to this. I'll tell you, we made sure that the nurse's aide was well taken care of for the rest of her life."

The elderly woman leaned forward and cupped my large black hand with her frail white hands. "Mr. Johnsson, you see, the nurse took our loneliness and brought us together so we could help others. You may feel lonely at times, but God has a special plan for you. What seems like a negative situation is God's opportunity for good."

CHAPTER 8

WHY WORRY?

YOU WILL CONTINUE TO live in the honor guard barracks. However, you will no longer report to any of the honor guard functions. Instead, you will report directly to me, the head of the public affairs office. And I report directly to the secretary of defense." While the Marine Corps major gave instructions to the new crew of Pentagon tour guides, I eyed the stack of 70-page handbooks perched on the corner of his desk. Would I ever be able to learn everything printed in that book? I'd applied and been accepted in the special training program for Pentagon tour guides.

"For the next two weeks you will walk the halls of the Pentagon to familiarize yourself with the different military corridors. When you lead the tours, you will walk backwards, so you'll have to have memorized the building layout."

"Backwards?"

The major anticipated my thoughts. "You walk backwards so that you can keep eye contact with the guests. We wouldn't want any unauthorized personnel wandering through sensitive areas of the complex. And don't worry—

the Pentagon staff know that they must stay out of your way, not the other way around."

The Pentagon tours began during President Carter's term, in 1976, for the country's bicentennial celebrations. They proved to be so popular that the government continued them. There were three tours: one for the general public, one for high school and political science students, and a third for visiting presidents and honored dignitaries from other countries. I would need to become familiar with all three. One corridor honored all those who'd received the Congressional Medal of Honor and other wartime medals. Next came the Time/Life Art corridor, where paintings and photographs taken during battles of World War II were displayed. Other corridors honored the five branches of the military.

I liked the commander in chief corridor the best. This one contained paintings of all of the United States presidents, and photographs highlighting their respective presidencies. I began collecting trivia on the presidents, little-known facts that would bring my presentations to life for the tourists. Because of my innate interest in American history, I became known as "Mr. Trivia" among the other tour guides.

One day I escorted some political science majors from one of the D.C. area colleges on the appropriate tour. As with most groups, the students found it fascinating that I could walk backwards and talk at the same time. In empty hallways where there were no exits and nothing of interest to talk about, I usually turned around and walked forward.

At one point that morning we entered such a hallway, and I spotted Lt. Col. Oliver North and his secretary, Fawn Hall, coming in our direction. Since the two of them had been appearing before Congress regarding the Iran-Contra hearing and they'd been interviewed on every network television news show, I knew the students would immediately recognize them.

What could I do? I glanced about for alternate directions could take my tour. There were none. I'd have to bluff it.

I took a deep breath, casually turned around, and walked forward, stepping up the pace, as if there were nothing of interest in that area of the building. I continued walking and talking until I was certain North and Hall had reached their destination. Then I turned around to continue my lecture and found myself totally alone. North, Hall, and 70 college students had vanished into the bowels of the Pentagon.

I panicked, dashing down one hallway after another. Finally I found my political science majors badgering Oliver North and his secretary with questions. Regaining my composure, I checked to be certain that all my lost sheep were accounted for. Then, adding a touch of military command to my voice, I herded them back down the corridor. The students gave me top grades for the tour, but I fear Oliver North and Fawn Hall wouldn't have been so generous.

Mr. Trivia didn't always score so well. One VIP tour included the chancellor of East Germany and his entourage. When I took him through the hallway with the World War II photographs, I pointed out with pride one photo taken of the largest bombing mission over Berlin during the war. A cloud passed over the faces of the chancellor's security men and the United States Secret Service men appointed to protect the dignitary.

The chancellor leaned close to the picture, then pointed at a badly scarred building in one corner. "By the way," he said, "during the bombing you described, my father was killed in that building right there."

The president's honor guard fills two posts at the Pentagon—tour guiding and sentry duty. My friend John was assigned to sentry duty. His job was to stand at the door to the office of the secretary of defense with a loaded .38 revolver on his hip.

As we prepared for our new assignments, John brought up the possibility of having to shoot someone. Both of us cringed at the thought of actually killing a person, even though we'd taken a vow to do so if necessary. John's problem remained theoretical until the morning that we hurried into the Pentagon's service personnel entrance by the Potomac River. Since I'd overslept and missed breakfast, I told John I wanted to grab a bite at the cafeteria before heading to the guard room.

"Wanna come?" I invited.

John glanced at his watch. "Can't. I go on duty in just a few minutes."

We rode the escalator to the second floor and split. I hurried toward the cafeteria, and John turned left toward Secretary of Defense Caspar Weinberger's office. Neither of us was aware that a young White male, upset over the United States' withdrawal of various trade restrictions on South Africa, had entered the building through the south entrance, intent on assassinating the secretary of defense. He carried a loaded .45 revolver.

The security guard asked to see the man's identification. The protester reached into his pocket as if to retrieve his wallet, then suddenly darted through the metal detector. He may have figured that with any luck he'd make it up to the defense secretary's office before being killed.

The metal detector sounded. The guards shouted for him to stop. He leaped onto the escalator. On the second floor, in front of the secretary's door, John stood poised, gun leveled at the next person to come off the escalator. I was on my way to the cafeteria when I heard shots. "Oh, no, John's been shot!" I screamed to myself, running toward the secretary's office.

Instead of jumping onto the up escalator, the gunman had jumped onto the down escalator, so it impeded his efforts in trying to go up. I rounded the corner just in time to see one of the guards shoot the intruder as he was stepping off the escalator at the top. He tumbled down the steps, coming to rest at the security guard's feet.

"Get back! Get back!" I shouted at the gawking office workers who hung over the stair railings. The guard at the foot of the stairs shouted, "Can somebody turn off the escalator?"

Later John and I talked. "How could that gunman have made such a stupid mistake as to leap onto the wrong escalator?" John mused. "A few seconds later I would have had to shoot him."

I nodded in agreement. "God tells us not to worry. He has everything under control."

Occasionally fractions of seconds can make the difference between success and disaster. Guiding a tour of senior citizens through the Time/Life Art corridor, I noticed that the office door of the sergeant major of the Army stood open. I warned my tour members, "Be very quiet as we pass the door to the office of the sergeant major of the United States Army. The sergeant major is working inside." I waved my arm in the direction of the door—just in time to connect with a cup of coffee in the sergeant major's hand.

My tour members gasped. I whirled about in panic as the hot liquid drenched the front of the startled sergeant major's shirt and pants. Grabbing a handkerchief from the hand of one of the alert tourists, I tried to wipe at the stain on the man's shirt. "So sorry, sir!"

"That's all right, airman. I guess you were so worried about keeping quiet for the Army's sergeant major that you ran into the sergeant major of the Army. Don't worry; I have another shirt in my office." The officer walked into his office and closed the door.

Somehow I made it through that tour and the next. As I prepared to leave at the end of the day, I received a note from office of the sergeant major of the Army. The note commended me for my exceptional conduct as a tour guide, and never mentioned the spilled coffee.

During my Pentagon duty I met and became friends with Tom, a United States Marines tour guide. We'd each been there only a short time when we learned that a new person was joining our staff, Erica. It would be my job to train her as a tour guide, and Tom's task to familiarize her with the Pentagon layout.

From the beginning, Tom and I made up our minds to win Erica's affections. We made a bet as to which of us she would date first. Erica caught on quickly to her good fortune. All she would have to do was say, "I'm so thirsty," and Tom and I would race to see who could fetch her a drink first. Or she'd coo, "I forgot to bring lunch money," and we'd both bring back a lunch from the commissary. We eagerly fulfilled her every wish, spending time and money, sending her flowers and candy. First, she'd act as though she preferred me, then it would be Tom, then me again. She had our heads spinning.

On the third weekend Erica announced that she had a visitor coming to see her. The visitor turned out to be her fiancé. The woman had played us both for fools. Fortunately it didn't damage the friendship between Tom and me.

My six-month tour of duty at the Pentagon ended. I knew I'd miss my time there. On the last day of our appointment, the duty sergeant called all the honor guards together. "Gentlemen, your service here at the Pentagon during the past six months has been exceptional," he said. "Each of you has done an excellent job representing the United States Armed Services and the honor guard. Secretary of Defense Caspar Weinberger has written letters of commendation for each of you. Copies will be included in your permanent file. Oh, yes, one more thing—I need to speak to the Black guy with the big mouth."

Immediately the other guards volunteered, "That's gotta be Johnsson." The sergeant looked at me. "Airman Johnsson, you need to report to the major's office immediately." As I walked to the major's office I reviewed in my mind all the possible errors I'd made during the past few months.

The major looked up from his desk when I followed his secretary into his office. "Stand at attention in front of me!"

"Yes, sir!"

The major eyed me thoughtfully for a moment. "According to our records, you have received four of the Tour Guide of the Month awards handed out during the past six months. This is highly unusual—unheard-of, actually—and the people in my office want to extend your service here at the Pentagon for a couple more months."

All the additional time I'd spent searching out historical trivia had paid off. The extra enthusiasm I put into my tours made them interesting for the visitors. As a result, I served in the Pentagon for nearly a year—another record.

I could never have brought about my extra-long stay at the Pentagon on my own, no matter how much I might have wanted it to happen. But God could and did. His plans for me so far had surpassed anything I might have imagined. And all He asked of me was to have faith in Him.

One night, after returning from a two-week leave, I checked my anemic bank account and realized that in order to make it to the end of the month and my next pay, I'd need to go to the bank and withdraw cash from my savings account. The next morning I walked to the credit union on the base and withdrew $60.

When I left the bank and counted the money, I brightened. I had $120! The cashier must have counted out my withdrawal twice. *Great,* I thought, *now I can cover all my bills.* "Thank You, Lord. I needed that!"

I walked back to the barracks feeling incredibly lucky. I forgot about the extra cash until I prepared for bed that night. I picked up my Bible and remembered the money stuffed in my wallet. "It's not yours, Terry," I told myself.

"Of course it is. This is the way God is solving my cash-flow problem." Throughout the night I argued with my conscience. By morning I knew what I had to do.

I rushed into the bank as the doors opened for business and asked to see the teller who'd been working line 5 the day before.

"You mean Mrs. Taylor," the older woman replied. "She's not available right now."

I persisted. "I must see her. It's very important."

"She's in counseling right now."

"What about?" I asked.

The woman looked at me indignantly. "I beg your pardon?"

"I must see the bank manager then."

"I'm sorry, sir, but that won't be possible either. That's who's speaking with Mrs. Taylor."

"Please forgive me, but I must insist." As I spoke I rushed toward the closed door marked Manager.

"Wait!" The woman hurried after me. "I'll tell him you're here." She disappeared into the office, closing the door behind her. The bank manager appeared a short time later. He looked irritated with me for interrupting his meeting. Behind him stood, tear-faced, the teller who had served me the day before.

"Sir," the manager began, "I am too busy right now to—"

I placed the envelope containing the extra $60 into his hand. "This won't take much of your time, sir. I believe this money is yours." Before I could complete my explanation Mrs. Taylor ran to hug me.

"Thank you, thank you so much. If you'd been 10 minutes later, I would have been fired," the teller sobbed. "I needed this job so desperately to support my year-old baby; my husband walked out on me three months ago. God bless you. God bless you."

How close I'd come to wrecking this young woman's career. I learned a lot about myself and my God that morning. How easy it would have been to keep the money and justify to myself that it was OK for me to do so. And about my God? I learned that He doesn't reward one of His children by injuring another.

Three days later the honor guard commander called me into his office and read me the letters he'd received from Mrs. Taylor and the bank manager. "You have done the honor guard proud, son. I've placed the letters in your permanent file."

At the next commander's call, the officer told the entire unit about the letters and then presented me with a step promotion, one that is seldom awarded during peacetime. The promotion allowed me to attend NCO (noncommissioned officer) training school, which would allow me to advance to the rank of sergeant. And just the first month's paycheck increase amounted almost to the penny what I'd almost kept from the bank!

Why worry? In his book *My Utmost for His Highest* Oswald Chambers wrote, "All fretting and worry comes from calculating without God" (p. 186).

All my worrying hadn't solved my problem. But if God can cover an IRS bill with a coin in a fish's mouth, He can certainly take care of my daily needs. God said, "Let not your heart be troubled." And He didn't mean just about money. He needed to teach me not to worry about any aspect of my life, including personal safety.

Between my military service and college I took a job as an inner-city youth Bible worker in southeast Washington, D.C., then known as one of the heaviest drug-use and crime areas in the United States. The assignment matched the one I had done in Portland while a teenager. I would knock on people's doors and ask them their needs and if I could do anything for them. However, my attitude differed from when I was in my teens. Now I truly wanted to help the people I met.

One morning I knocked on a door in a housing project, a rough neighborhood. As I waited for an answer, I felt that someone was watching me. The door opened enough to allow a rifle barrel to slide through, aimed directly at my chest.

A cold calculating voice beyond the door said, "I don't know who you are, but if you move I'll shoot you." I stiffened, and considered backing away until I felt a second gun pressed against my back.

Scared? You know I was scared. Worried? Oh, yeah! I took a deep breath and prayed. Suddenly I said something out loud that shocked my two assailants and me—"Let go, and let God take control."

The guy inside the house opened the door and looked at me as if I were crazy. I'd unwittingly knocked on the door of the neighborhood's head drug lord. The man growled, "What did you say?"

I gulped and repeated myself.

He jabbed the gun into my chest. "Man, what in the world are you talking about? I could shoot you right now."

"Well, sir, I've learned that when I face difficult situations, God wants me to turn it all over to Him, and that's just what I did."

"Are you saying that God is going to get you out of this jam you're in?"

"Friend, I am simply realizing that there is nothing I can do. If you want to shoot me, I can't do anything about it. But if God doesn't want you to shoot me, you won't be able to."

"Is that a challenge?"

Before I could reply, the man at my back jabbed his gun against my backbone. "Man, we need to hurry up and get rid of him."

I braced myself for the bullet. Instead, the man in front of me lowered his rifle and squinted up at me. "You must be one of those Christians."

"Yes, sir, I am. And I'm here in the neighborhood to find people who might have specific needs that I and my organization might be able to fill."

The man wrinkled his face and waved the gun in the air. "G'wan, get out of here! I don't want to see you anymore."

The next morning when I returned to the neighborhood, I learned that the word had gone out: "Don't mess with the young Black Bible worker while he's working our turf. You let him do his thing."

Punks, drug dealers, and prostitutes obeyed the guy's warning, even though my presence hurt their business. As a result, I could go anywhere and talk to anyone in the neighborhood in total safety.

Did I change this man's mind? Hardly. If I'd been on my own, I would have either fainted or screamed for the police. Both actions would have ended in a much less desirable way.

No fear. Kids wear T-shirts and baseball caps blazoned with these two brave words, yet they walk the streets of their neighborhoods in constant terror for their lives. God has the answer for that fear. I know. I've seen it work.

CHAPTER 9

DREAM THE DREAM

A COLD ARCTIC BREEZE STUNG the tips of my ears as I stood in formation with the other members of the president's honor guard at 1600 Pennsylvania Avenue. Fifty state flags rippled above our heads. I gripped the pole supporting the Wyoming state flag with my gloved hand. Another day, another ceremony. I swallowed the yawn forming in the back of my throat and stared at a place far beyond the heads of the assembled guests and reporters.

As the prime minister of Australia looked on, President Reagan expounded upon America's friendship with the land down under, and the future of our countries in the world market.

My thoughts switched to my own uncertain future. Earlier that day the guard commander had spoken to me about signing up for another tour of duty. I knew I couldn't stay in the honor guard forever. Was it time for me to move on? If so, to where? To do what? *What should I do with the rest of my life?* I wondered.

I thought about the people who had shown an interest in

my future—my grandmother Settles' prophecy that I'd be a preacher . . . Commissioner Schwab's prediction that I'd be a member of Portland's city council by the time I reached 30 . . . and old Mr. Johnston.

I remembered how frightened I was the day I reported to the military processing center in downtown Portland. Mr. Johnston met me at the door. He handed me the forms I needed to fill out, then gave me a strange look. Later I learned that he'd been handing out processing forms at the center for 40 years. I also learned that the 300 or so recruits being processed that day for the five branches of the military would be the last group to go through the center at that location—it was being moved to a new million-dollar facility.

At the door to the room where we'd be given our physical exams, Mr. Johnston met me again—and again he handed me a form and gave me a strange, quizzical look.

Great, I thought, *I'm not even in the Air Force yet and they don't like me.* As I started to enter the room Mr. Johnston spoke to me. "At the end of the day I'd like to speak with you, son. Make sure you're alone."

My eyes narrowed as I studied the craggy old face. Maybe they're going to throw me out before I even enter . . . Maybe they found my school records and . . . I could only imagine. As I inched through the induction process my mind raced. Why in the world would they want me, anyway ? Maybe I should just turn around and go home.

When the eight-hour induction process ended, I thought, *Maybe he forgot about me.* But no such luck. Before I could make good my escape, Mr. Johnston spotted me and waved me into his office. Once inside, he said, "I've been working this job for many years, and I've processed thousands of guys. I've gotten to the point where I can tell the good guys from the bad ones. I can tell that you're one of the good ones. And I have this strange feeling that you are going to rise in the military."

Surprised, I managed to mumble a thank-you.

"Whatever you're doing with your life, keep it up," he added.

Stumbling around for a reply, I said, "I've just recently become a Christian."

He cast me a wry smile. "I'm not a religious person myself, but I get good vibes from you. When you come home on leave, drop by and let me know how you're doing, to see if my hunch is right."

I mumbled a promise to do as he asked, and shook his hand. Outside the building I shook my head and thought, *That's strange! I joined the Air Force in order to make attending college a possibility, not to make it my life's career.*

In academy my fellow classmates had discussed their exciting dreams and goals and where they could put their talents to best use. But me? What talents did I have? Goals? I barely planned beyond eating lunch at McDonald's with my buddies. I certainly didn't have any compelling dreams on which to focus. Matter of fact, I couldn't see any real future for myself. What could I contribute to society? My desire to excel and my lack of direction caused my friendships to seesaw between those students who were motivated and those just drifting. More often I found myself with the drifting crowd. My joining the Air Force had been the result of a coin toss—I would go to college with the motivated kids or enlist in the military with a couple buddies. Later my buddies changed their minds, leaving me a lone inductee in the United States Air Force.

While my experiences in flight training and the police academy proved to be challenging, my experience in the honor guard supplied a positive foundation upon which I could build my future.

But as I stood on the White House lawn that frigid December afternoon, I considered my options and thought about the advice I'd received from others. I still didn't know what Terry Johnsson wanted for Terry Johnsson. A part of me wanted to remain secure with the successes I'd had. Another part of me yearned to see beyond the military.

I recalled a recent phone call I'd made to Grandma Settles. I told her of my perplexities.

"Terry," she said, "I'm ashamed of you. You've let the devil get hold of your dreams and confuse you." Leave it to my grandmother to hit the nail on the head. "Maybe so, Grandma. So how do I change that?"

"You need to ask God to help you dream again."

"Is that it?" My logical mind looked askance at my loved one's simplistic advice.

"No, not quite. After you pray, imagine that the president of the United States comes up to you and asks you, 'What do you want to do with your life? I am here to help and support you in any way I can.' Then he adds, 'Don't dream small dreams. Dream something big, something you really want to do.'"

That's my grandma, I laughed to myself. *Her dreams are never small.*

Then Grandma added, "Now, instead of the president of the Unites States, picture the King of the universe saying the same thing and promising to help you reach your God-given goals by supplying you with everything you could possibly need."

I thanked her, then hung up. My intellect scoffed—*too easy.* Yet Grandma had been right about so many things over the years.

As I stood in formation that blustery day on the balcony of the White House portico, I mentally listed all the possibilities I'd considered over the years. I narrowed my dreams down to three possibilities—to be a preacher, stay with the military, or become a politician.

I'd received several offers from major players on the Washington, D.C., scene, promising that if I were interested they would set me up with scholarships and start my life in politics. My superiors in the honor guard encouraged me to make a career out of the military. "With your record you can go anywhere you want in the service, Johnsson."

General Colin Powell called another guardsman and me aside in the cafeteria. He told us that for an African-American to rise in the military, a college education would be helpful. "Get your degree. You'll need it if you plan to make the military your career."

Pastor friends urged me to study for the ministry. Not only would I be helping people, they said, but I'd be sharing God's Word as well. I knew I wanted to help people in a special way. I enjoyed working with teenagers. I could see that college would be the next step, regardless of my career choice. But, most important, I knew that satisfaction and happiness comes from being exactly where God wants you to be.

Now, you might say, "What's the big quandary here? God is going to lead you to become a minister. That's His business."

No, that's not necessarily true. Not everyone is cut out to be a preacher or a doctor or a garage mechanic. Inherited talents and interests are ours for a purpose—God's purpose. God uses people in different positions to glorify Him, not just in positions connected directly with church work. One service is no less important than another if you are where God wants you to be.

I recalled talking with my grandma about dreams and finding one's future. Her advice was "Test your dreams."

"Test my dreams, Grandma? How?"

She smiled. "There are three tests I use. First, will my dream help other people? Second, does my dream fit into harmony with God's plan? And third, when God blesses me as I carry out that dream, will I give Him the credit? If you can answer yes to all these questions, you're on your way."

"Even the impossible dreams?" I asked, partly teasing.

"Dreams that seem impossible are not impossible with God," she replied.

My mother has become a terrific example of reaching for impossible dreams. Mother always wanted to be an inspirational speaker. People kept telling her that such a dream was impossible because of her southern Creole accent. At 61, after six children and eight grandchildren, she gave her dream to God. Today she travels across the United States sharing the story of God's goodness in her life. Her heavy speaking itinerary would put a traveling evangelist to shame. Recently both of our names were on the list to speak at a graduation exercise. The committee chose her over me and over 12 other candidates.

But that day on the White House lawn, while I hadn't a clue how I should dream, it was clear that college should be my next move. An inner voice nagged at my decision. "Terry, you can't! You're too . . ." I shut off the negative recordings. Right after that, I began putting my plans into motion. I made arrangements with my commander to be released early in order to help with an inner-city program in the months before I headed for college in the fall. I would stay in the guard until after the Bush inauguration.

Incoming JEEPs handled the inauguration proceedings because the old-timers preferred to cover the farewell for the outgoing president, their last chance to serve their commander in chief. President Reagan had been particularly pro-military during his terms in office, so it was a special honor for the five branches of service to attend his farewell ceremony.

Having secured the status of sergeant months previously, I was appointed NCO in charge of the event. It was my job to be certain that government dignitaries and their spouses, military brass and their spouses, foreign ambassadors, cabinet members, members of the Air Force band, and members of the press—more than 600 people—were directed to their correct reserved seats inside a gigantic aircraft hangar. Surrounding the seating area, United States *Air Force One* and the president's helicopter, as well as a sample of each of the planes and helicopters approved during the Reagan administration, were parked. The Coast Guard displayed samples of their newest drug-fighting boats.

The press box on the far side of the dais concerned me the most. I stood at the end of the front line closest to the dais so I could keep my eye on the press box. I didn't want any eager-beaver photojournalists trying to stretch the parameters of their privilege.

Chills ran the length of my spine when the Air Force band struck the first chords of "Hail to the Chief." Just as President Reagan started down the corridor of honor guards, a photographer distracted me for a moment. By the time I returned my attention to the president, he was less than three feet from me. Instinctively I snapped off a salute. To my surprise and to the delight of the audience, President Reagan returned my salute. The crowd erupted into cheers and applause at the commander in chief's unplanned gesture.

Reagan continued his walk to the dais to the standing ovation of the crowd. He raised his hand to silence their applause. Tears brimmed in the retiring president's eyes as he spoke of his years as commander in chief. Before he left the hangar, he turned to the gathered assembly and shouted, "I'm proud of you all."

Later, alone in my room, I looked back over my years in the White House honor guard. In less than four years I'd met more heads of state than had any member of Congress. I never dreamed God would take me so far in so little time. Grandma Settles was right—my dreams had been too small.

On the day of George Bush's inauguration a biting January

wind whipped through the swearing-in area. My staff and I had been making last-minute adjustments since 4:00 a.m. I scanned the scene, knowing that in a very short time the procession would arrive and George Bush would be sworn in as president of the United States.

I started in surprise at the sudden sound of laughing and talking. Children rambled out onto the platform. The Bushes' grandkids had arrived. Then the president-to-be came onto the platform. He took time to bend down and listen to a younger grandchild. Mrs. Bush helped round them all up, even patting down a cowlick on one of the boys. Family and neighbors of the Bushes gathered side by side with U.S. senators and several of the nation's religious leaders—Robert Schuller, Billy Graham, and Norman Vincent Peale.

I told my friend Sergeant Griffey how impressed I was with the family atmosphere.

"Like the Carter inauguration," he confided. "President Reagan's inauguration was more high-class."

I studied the face of the president's mother. It shone with pride and determination. I thought of my own mother back in Oregon, and the determination she had for the kid who couldn't read. I felt as though I would burst my buttons with gratitude that day.

When Reagan turned over the presidency to Bush, I felt akin to him. Leaving the honor guard was proving to be much more difficult than I'd imagined. I listened as the new president said, "The new breeze blows, a page turns, the story unfolds—and so today a chapter begins . . ."

For me also a new chapter would begin. I would face my demons head-on—I would go back to school.

CHAPTER 10

Beginnings and Endings

DURING THE SUMMER MONTHS before entering college, I worked in the inner city of Washington, D.C. It was there that I discovered that dreams are like cherry pits. In every pit lies a tree waiting to grow to its full potential and to give fruit, which in time will produce more pits, and so forth.

When I was a kid, our family traveled to Louisiana to visit family. I couldn't believe my eyes when I saw a tree full of ripe cherries. I'd never seen anything like that. In Portland, Oregon, where I grew up, we had to go to a store to buy cherries, and they were very expensive—or at least they seemed so to a small boy.

When we returned home, I asked my father if he would buy a cherry tree for me. He laughed. "Son, we live in the city. A cherry tree won't grow here."

I looked as though I'd cry, and he laughed again. "Maybe you could go to the library and find a book on growing cherry trees in the city."

I took him at his word. I wanted my very own cherry tree.

I found a book at my school library that told me how to help a seed grow. Soon after, I visited my aunt's home and learned that she had a cherry tree in her backyard. I picked five or six cherries, ate the fruit, then stuffed the pits in my jeans pocket. When I got home, I did exactly as the book said on how to plant seeds. To the surprise of everyone, including me, two of the pits sprouted. Following the book's instructions exactly, I transplanted the two plants to the backyard.

It wasn't long afterward that my father died and our family moved to another house. Years later I returned to the first house and discovered a 20-foot cherry tree growing in the backyard. I joined the neighborhood kids in eating cherries from that tree.

My dreams, like trees nestled within cherry pits, were just waiting for the right circumstances in which to grow. If I'd kept the seeds in my pants pocket instead of planting them, the life within them would have shriveled and died. I had to plant them in rich soil so they could grow. Washington's inner city proved to be the right soil in which my dreams could grow.

My supervisor assigned a young academy student for me to train. He reminded me of myself. He noted how I approached the residents of the area, looking for ways we could help them fill their needs.

Every day on our way to and from "the projects," we walked past Barbara. Barbara began her day in front of the local liquor store. The neighborhood wino, she lived to drink. Leaning against a corner telephone pole, she'd guzzle down the strongest drink she could afford and talk with everyone who drove by or walked past the pole. By noon she'd be slumping a little farther down the pole, but still talking and waving to the passersby. By midafternoon Barbara would be out cold on the ground.

One day my young friend said, "Terry, you're always talking so positively to everyone. Can't you do anything for Barbara?"

Ouch! How can you get through to a rum-soaked brain?

The people in the neighborhood had never seen a time Barbara was sober. I remembered what Robert Schuller had once said, that God could work on the subconscious mind. *OK,* I thought, *I'll take Robert Schuller at his word and see what happens.*

The next day on my way home from work, I found Barbara passed out on the sidewalk. I stopped, bent down, and held her hand in mine. "Barbara, God loves you, and so do I."

I felt foolish, as though I were talking to myself. My young friend watched, but said nothing. I rose to my feet and headed home. The next day I did the same, and the next and the next. Before long my friend was kneeling down beside me, and both of us were repeating the simple words "God loves you, and so do I."

A morning came when we didn't find Barbara drinking by her telephone pole. I wondered where she might have gone. When I asked, no one seemed to know. Days and weeks passed—no Barbara. Secretly I suspected that the booze had gotten the best of her, that she'd either died from liver damage or been killed by a passing vehicle.

At the end of the summer we held a series of meetings on living a more healthful lifestyle. We invited the entire neighborhood. One evening at the end of the meeting a program assistant approached me and said there was a woman who wanted to speak with me. "She looks a little angry," the assistant confided.

Oh, great, I thought. *Whom have I managed to offend?* Getting on the wrong side of the wrong person in this neighborhood could be deadly. But before I could respond, an attractive, well-dressed woman strode toward me. From her salon-styled hair to her perfectly applied makeup she represented the epitome of class. She drew closer and pointed at me. "I heard you've been talking about me."

I cleared my throat and widened my eyes. "Ma'am, do I know you?" She looked vaguely familiar.

I've been told that you're the one who's been putting that 'God loves you' in my mind."

My mouth dropped open in surprise. "Barbara? You're Barbara?"

The woman told me her story. "When I could finally struggle to my feet, I would hear over and over in my mind, 'God loves you, Barbara; God loves you.' When I took a shower, when I ate breakfast, I would hear your words again and again: 'God loves you.'" She paused and studied my face for several seconds. I searched for something to say, but could think of nothing.

"It got to the point where your words were driving me crazy. I had to find out who was playing this sick joke on me."

I admit that when I first spoke those words in Barbara's ear I expected nothing. I never would have guessed that the drunken woman vomiting on the street corner would one day clean up her act and find her way to a church, which she attended until her death.

While I was helping in a rough neighborhood in New York City, a friend of mine gave me a Christian rap tape. "Listen to this, Terry. It's a new type of Christian music."

I told him thank you and stuck the tape in my pocket. Rap, Christian or otherwise, wasn't my type of music. I forgot about the tape; then one afternoon I came upon a group of teenage boys—10 to 15 of them—sitting on a street corner and harassing the people walking by.

As I drew near to the corner, one of the leaders accosted me. "What are you doing here? You're always coming around here with your Bible in your hand. You think you're better than we are, don't you?"

Instead of answering, I remembered the tape in my pocket. "Hey, I just remembered that I have a gift for you."

I handed him the tape and continued on my way.

The next morning I parked my car and got out to find myself immediately surrounded by the same bunch of boys. I stiffened, thinking that they were intending to beat me up. The leader moved into my face. "Hey, man, where in the world did you get that tape? It's the best tape I've ever heard. The words are so real, so down-to-earth. I never heard anyone talk about God that way. Can you get us some more?"

Could I? You bet. I never would have guessed that God could use for His glory the rap tape that I'd intended to trash. The leader and 21 of his friends attended my meetings and are still living lives devoted to God.

Experiences like these caused my dreams to sprout and grow. I realized that if I became a pastor I could satisfy all three of my desires at the same time. I could help people, work with teenagers, and share my love for God.

When I entered college in the fall, I kept quiet about my honor guard past. Being slightly older than my classmates already set me somewhat apart. I needed to study to keep up, because I'd elected to take two majors at the same time—religion and communications.

I began dating a girl I was certain would become my wife. We dated throughout my first three years in college. I traveled on weekends, speaking at various churches and youth conferences around the country. At first she enjoyed my notoriety; later her enjoyment turned to tolerance.

It was during my senior year that what became a famous phone call came into the school's main switchboard. News that the White House was calling Terry Johnsson to assist at the Clinton inauguration spread across the college campus before it reached me. I was in the Air Force Reserves, so my friend Sergeant Griffey had decided to use me for the upcoming inaugurations.

I arrived at the honor guard barracks and seemed to drop

back in time—all the old familiar scenes. But the people had changed. The only man other than Sergeant Griffey who had served with me was Sergeant Ali. He'd advanced to one of the top positions in the office.

"Terry, I'd like you to come outside and meet the troops," Ali invited.

"Sure, I'd like that."

He took me outside and announced to the assembled men, "I'd like to introduce to you the famous Sergeant Terry Johnsson."

I gaped in amazement as whispers skittered throughout the ranks. One of the braver guards asked, "This is the real Terry Johnsson? We thought you guys had made him up."

When Sergeant Ali dismissed the men, they rushed up to me.

"Did you really . . . ?" And the questions began. "We thought for sure they had made you up." I had been out of the guard for four years, and it seemed these young guys knew more about my adventures than I remembered myself.

Sergeant Ali told me later that I'd been asked to return to visit in order to boost morale and so that I could tell them all about the Bush inauguration. He also allowed me to inspect the troops one last time.

Sergeant Griffey assigned me the task of checking the marching of the Air Force personnel at the inaugural proceedings. I would stand next to Harry Smith, of *CBS This Morning*. I watched the new president greet the troops. When he reached me, President Bill Clinton shook my hand and looked me straight in the eye. "Hello," he said.

"I pray that God will bless your term as president," I replied. He smiled and moved on to the next person in line.

I returned to campus to learn that there were very few job openings that spring for ministerial interns. No job? I'd never considered such a possibility. I prayed, "Lord, You brought me this far and now there's no job? How can that be?"

I called my girl and told her the bad news. "We need to pray about this, since it affects both our futures." Soon after, I discovered that it didn't affect the future of both of us. My numerous speaking engagements around the country were something that she didn't want to live with for the rest of her life. We decided to call quits on our relationship.

I knew that our breakup would have a double impact on my future; not only did I love the woman, but also in the Seventh-day Adventist Church the officials want their ministers to be married.

Mailing out more than 30 job résumés, I purposely didn't mention my background in the White House. I wanted to be hired for my ministering skills. For that matter, up until the phone call from the White House, many people on campus didn't know about my service there, either. I did everything I could to find placement, and kept on praying.

I took a trip back to Portland during spring break and went to visit my old neighborhood. I ran into a woman named Martha from my old church. We talked for some time about the neighborhood and where everyone had gone.

"The old neighborhood has changed, Terry. The gangs have taken over Portland. And I'm worried about little Gary. I don't know how long he can hold out from joining."

Gary was a mutual friend, a kid with great potential for good. I remembered the neighborhood gangs from my youth, mainly just a bunch of kids trying to act tough like their favorite TV action heroes. "If you'd like, I'll talk with him," I offered.

"Would you?" Martha beamed with delight.

"Sure, I'd be glad to. Tell you what, why don't you round up the guys and bring them all to my mom's place? My mother loves to cook her great Southern food for company. I figure we can eat and play some games, and I can talk to them about the neighborhood problems."

Fear and confusion filled Martha's eyes. "Are you sure? You're asking me to bring the Crips to your mother's house?" She shook her head slowly. "I don't think that would be a very good idea."

I assured her that I'd spoken to young people all over the world and I could handle a bunch of kids who called themselves a weird name such as the Crips. "They're just a bunch of kids who've watched too many scary movies about gangs."

Later that day I ran across a friend from another downtown Portland neighborhood. I told her how that night I would be talking with a bunch of kids at my mom's home in Troutdale, a small community outside Portland. I believed that getting them away from their neighborhoods would give them a new perspective.

"Really? There are some kids in my neighborhood who are in a gang too. I wish you could talk with them as well. They call themselves the Bloods."

"Why not?" I gestured magnanimously. "Bring them along. We'll have a great time together."

"Are you sure you know what you are doing?"

"No problem."

"Won't your mother mind?"

"Absolutely not. My mom's cool with stuff like this."

"OK, if you're sure."

On the phone I cleared my little get-together with my mother. My mother simpered, "Oh, Terry, that's so sweet of you. You should be resting. You're on vacation, remember?"

"Thanks, Mom, but this will be like a rest for me. Oh, by the way, these kids call themselves the Bloods."

"Say what?"

"I said these kids—"

"I know what you said, son, but do you know what you said?"

"Of course. I said—"

"Terry! You can't bring these thugs into our home."

"Mother, don't worry."

"Don't worry? Just last week the Bloods killed some people in North Portland."

I clicked my tongue. "Mother, these are little kids from the old neighborhood. Oh, yes, and by the way, I ran into Martha from church, and she's bringing a group of children who call themselves the Crips." I heard her drop the phone.

When she retrieved it, I could hear fear in her voice. "Terry, the Crips and the Bloods fight and kill each other."

"Mom, these are only young children who need a little guidance. There are none of the real gangs in Portland. Don't worry. I'll see you tonight."

The moment I hung up the phone, my mother called all the deacons of the church and asked them to come over to her place that night. She called all the pastors in the area and asked them the same thing. Then she called the Troutdale Police Department, warning them to be on alert should she need to make an emergency call to them that evening.

Back in Portland, and separate of one another, the Crips and the Bloods heard they'd been offered a ride out to the little country town of Troutdale for a free Southern meal. Sounded great to them.

When I returned to my folks' place, more than 20 cars lined the gravel driveway. I knew the kids wouldn't be coming for more than an hour. I walked into the house and found more than 30 people there, moving furniture around, hiding my mother's breakable treasures. My mother had already hidden the VCR. Some of them frowned when they saw me, as if thinking, *How could you do this to your mother?*

Before I could react, I heard a school bus coming up the driveway. I whirled about and hurried outside to greet the little kids getting off the bus. I stared in surprise to discover these were not little kids. These were tough young people in their teens and 20s. My mouth hung open as 25 Bloods climbed off the bus.

I welcomed them and told them to go ahead inside and downstairs to the family room. They'd barely disappeared inside the house when two vans pulled up and 22 Crips climbed out—there was not a little kid in sight.

"What have I gotten into this time, Lord?" I scratched my head, shrugged my shoulders, and invited them inside the house as well.

The instant the first Crip entered my mother's house, he spotted the Bloods. Shouting and cursing followed. The gang members hauled out their weapons from their pockets, readying for a fight. I took a deep breath and jumped into the middle of it, shouting over their noise. "OK, I need five of the Crips' best pool players." One boy called out a name. "Raise your hand," I shouted. "You play a good game of pool?"

Other hands followed. "Now I need five of the Bloods' best pool players. We're going to have a playoff tournament. Whoever wins will get to eat Zelma's Southern cookin' first." I added, "We have Nintendo and table soccer. Do we have any takers?" I waved them toward the stairs. "Come on, let's play pool."

The gang members looked around nervously, waiting for someone to make a move. Finally one leader from each gang gave the OK, and the kids surged down the stairs.

By the time my mother brought on the food, deacons and preachers stared in amazement to see the gang members laughing and having a great time together.

Instead of talking to the entire group at the same time, God impressed me to talk with them one on one. Before the night ended, I'd talked and prayed with 47 gang members. Some of them broke down in tears. They begged me not to tell the others they'd been crying. Of the 47, 20 decided that night to leave their gang.

After hearing my story, they said, "If God can use you and change your life, maybe He can do the same for me."

One young man named Bo told me that if he could get a job he'd leave the gangs. He promised to look for work. When I got back to school I learned that the boy had been executed by his own gang. He knew too much for them to let him live.

At the boy's funeral, his mother said, "I don't know what came over my son the last few weeks of his life, but he changed. He started going to church with me. I found him reading his Bible. He told me he was calling the schools in the area. He wanted to finish his GED." She went on to say, "I always knew he was going to die young. But thank God, he turned his life around before he did."

Following Bo's death several neighborhood young people left the gangs. Whenever I visit those neighborhoods, I hear young people call me and ask, "Pastor Terry, do you remember me?" And I remember the time God used my stupidity for His glory. Isn't God incredible?

I returned to Oakwood for the last quarter of my senior year, still with no job prospects. That's when I received an invitation from Don Jacobsen, president of the Oregon Conference of Seventh-day Adventists. They'd heard about my encounter with the gangs and had chosen to offer me the position of youth pastor. When I reported for duty to Pastor Jacobsen, I was shocked to learn that I would be pastoring at the Stone Tower church in Portland. The senior pastor, Phil Shultz, a Marine officer during the Vietnam war, had requested me.

I laughed. Two years earlier I'd been invited to speak at

that church. After I gave my message, I told my mother and my niece Shannon that I'd love to pastor there someday. Shannon chuckled and reminded me that the church had an all-White congregation.

When I arrived in Portland, I discovered that a White supremacist group had set up a skinhead gang immediately behind the Stone Tower church. They'd killed a Black man on the streets of the city a few months earlier.

My first task at my new assignment was to conduct a "can drive" in the neighborhood to build up the supply of food for the homeless. My partner, David Prictard, and I started going door to door, unaware that the skinheads had several houses in the neighborhood. At one door we read a large sign: "White Power!" Since the door was partly open and no one came to answer the bell, I peeked inside. A poster of Adolf Hitler stared back at me from the wall opposite the door. Next to the poster hung a KKK flag.

"Oh, boy," I muttered, "am I in big trouble." I told David to take a look as well; just then the door swung open. Out stepped a six-foot-two-inch startled skinhead. We stood nose to nose, neither of us knowing quite what to say.

"You know this is a skinhead group home?" he sputtered, his gaze darting about nervously.

I was equally as nervous. Instead of saying something profound or even responding to his question, I repeated my set speech. "I'm Pastor Terry Johnsson, and this is my friend, David. We're Christians, and we're collecting canned foods for the homeless."

The man continued to stare at me, uncertain what to do next. I glanced toward David's ashen face and realized he was as unnerved as I. The man recovered enough to tell us to stay where we were, that he'd be right back.

Now, I was ready to leave the moment the man disappeared

inside the home. David shook his head. "Let's wait and see what happens."

Wait and see what happens? That was easy for David to say. He was White. My knees shook and my hand trembled when the skinhead returned with an armful of canned food and dropped them into my grocery bag. He looked a little uncomfortable and added, "I wish we had more."

I inhaled sharply, pasted on a smile, and thanked him. "God bless you," I added. The moment I said "God bless you," he started as if someone had dumped a bucket of icy water over his head. He looked at us as if to say, "What have I done? Giving food to a Black Christian pastor?"

We walked down the porch steps and onto the sidewalk while the man stood in his doorway shaking his shaved head in disbelief.

I moved into an apartment next door to the church. My neighbors began greeting me with "Hi, Pastor Terry." They came to me for counseling and to conduct their weddings and funerals. For four years I was their resident pastor.

During the 1996 presidential election campaign President Clinton visited Portland. My friends and I decided to attend the rally. It brought back all kinds of memories, walking through the metal detectors and past uniformed Secret Service agents. At the checkpoints I wondered why the security officers looked at me so strangely. But when none of us were stopped, I forgot about it.

Our entire group managed to get up close to the front of the audience. We stood waiting to see the president arrive when two Secret Service agents came up to me and asked me if I was Terry Johnsson. My friends were shocked to see the agents march me away. They thought I must have done something terribly wrong. And I wasn't too sure I hadn't been confused with some criminal on the run. I shouted back to my friends, "Don't worry. I'm sure it must be some mistake."

The agents took me to a guarded area and told me to sit down on one of the chairs. A top agent entered the room and asked, "Are you Sergeant Terry Johnsson?"

"Yes, sir," I replied.

"I told you I'd get you back someday, Sarge."

"Bill!" Now it was my turn to be shocked. Bill and I had served in the guard together. In fact, I had trained him. And now he was a member of Clinton's Secret Service team. We had a great time catching up on everything that had happened since we left the honor guard. They told me what they were doing, and I told them about my escapades as a youth pastor.

When it was time for the rally to begin, Bill and several of the Secret Service men walked me back to my friends. We embraced and said goodbye. With tears in his eyes Bill added, "It was so good to see you again. I'll tell the fellows that you are finally living your dream."

On the way home my friends admitted they'd sometimes doubted that all my government stories were true. Had I really met all the famous people I talked about, and had I done all the things I said? My Secret Service friends gave them all the proof they needed to believe.

Shortly after arriving in Oregon to pastor, I received a message from a friend in the honor guard. He said that he would be in Yorba Linda, California, for the funeral of Richard Nixon. "Would you like to fly down for a visit?"

Would I? I cleared the trip with the senior pastor and with my church leaders. I knew it would seem strange being there yet not part of the guard. I never imagined the trip would turn out so beneficial for me.

I went straight from the airport to the hotel, then to the memorial service. As I entered the garden area where the service was being held, I glanced about in awe. I'd never seen so many important people gathered in one place. At the end of the service, people filed out to attend a private reception. Seeing Robert Schuller walk by blew my mind. During my freshman year of college I had read every book I could find by Norman Vincent Peale and Robert Schuller. Each week I had watched the *Hour of Power* on television.

One night my roommate heard me talking in my sleep. According to him, I said, "Let me open the door for you." Then I started laughing.

My roommate awakened me. "Terry, you were dreaming you were back at the White House."

I shook the last vestiges of sleep from my mind. "No, I wasn't at the White House. I had the strangest dream, that I was talking to Robert Schuller and got to open a door for him."

Now it was my roommate's turn to laugh. "Terry, you'd better stop watching that program."

And now, three years later, I gathered up my courage and walked up to Schuller and his wife at the Nixon funeral. I introduced myself, and we shook hands. I asked how late the prayer chapel at the Crystal Cathedral was open at night.

"All night," Schuller responded. "Just tell the guards that you want to pray, and they'll let you into the chapel."

I thanked him and headed back to my rental car. After dining, I returned to my hotel room, intending to get to bed early for a change. But I couldn't sleep, thinking about the events of the day. At 11:30 p.m. I decided to drive to the Crystal Cathedral and spend some time in the prayer chapel.

I found the parking lot empty except for a Mercedes parked in the handicapped space. After parking my rental, I strode over to the chapel to pray. I had felt like such an outsider that day as I watched my guard friends carry out their military duties. Questions had rambled through my mind. Did I make the right choice in leaving the honor guard? If

I'd stayed with the guard, where would I be by now? My friend said he could get me back in the Air Force if I wanted. *Maybe the guard is where I belong,* I decided.

I left the chapel and was nearing the parking lot when a limousine pulled up and two people got out. As I got closer, I realized they were Robert Schuller and his wife; they were leaving the limo for the parked Mercedes. Delighted to see them again, I went up and shook the surprised minister's hand.

"I met you at the service today," I reminded him. We talked for a few minutes while Mrs. Schuller climbed into the driver's seat of the Mercedes. Schuller asked me what I did for a living.

"I used to be in the president's honor guard, but now I'm a youth pastor in Oregon." Schuller looked me straight in the eyes and said, "God has brought you this far. He wants you to stay in the ministry and work for Him."

My eyes widened. I gulped. How did he know I was considering leaving the ministry?

As he turned toward the car door, he invited, "Why don't you come by tomorrow and take a tour of the facilities here?"

I reached for the door handle and said, "Let me get that for you, Dr. Schuller."

I stared after the Mercedes as the Schullers drove out of the parking lot. "This has happened before," I mumbled aloud. I began to laugh. Won't my ex-roommate be surprised?

If I hadn't gone to the prayer chapel, if I hadn't connected with Robert Schuller that evening, if he hadn't said what he said to me, I would have called certain people the next morning to begin the process of reenlisting in the Air Force.

"God has brought you this far." Schuller's words haunted my sleep that night. The next day I returned to tour the grounds of the Crystal Cathedral. As he and I posed together for pictures, I thanked him for his counsel.

Today I am so glad I have stayed in the ministry. God has taken me around the world to 50 states and more than 60 countries. I've told my story to thousands, young and old, rich and poor, famous and ordinary.

In life we may choose our roads, thinking we know where they will take us, but no one knows for sure at the beginning of a journey where life's road will take them. No one can predict the muddy roads or the detours they will encounter along the way. I've learned as I've traveled over bumpy roads and smooth highways that if I let God do the driving, I can expect the incredible to happen.

I don't know what roads God and I will travel tomorrow, the next day, or the next. Regardless, wherever He takes me, I plan to tighten my seat belt and enjoy the ride.

EPILOGUE

TERRY LYNDON JOHNSSON currently serves as a pastor in Takoma Park, Maryland, just outside Washington, D.C. He is a sought-after speaker, and has traveled extensively throughout both the United States and the world, including the former U.S.S.R., telling fascinating stories and sharing the good news. He hosts a weekly radio program, *Real Issues,* and serves as radio pastor on WGTS (91.9 FM), a nonprofit organization that provides Christian music to the Washington, D.C., area. Recently he helped organize a Saturday night church service for the New Community Fellowship in the Washington area.